Stella

D1274432

FIVE
MINUTES
to
IMPACT

David Osborne is a true business entrepreneur. He is a value-based businessman. David is also a skillful, experienced private airplane pilot. This is the story of a pilot's worst fears lived out! As a private pilot myself, I caught myself mentally following the story . . . a story of a miracle landing on a dark night with seemingly nowhere to land. Dave tells the story from his perspective—a faith-based worldview intertwined in every aspect of his life. I'm sure that you, like me, will not be able to put down this incredible story. If you know a pilot, give this book to her or him for an inspirational experience.

—LAUREN LIBBY
International President/CEO, TWR International

I have known David Osborne for over thirty years. He's meticulous and careful in every part of life. As a pilot, he used those skills to save his and others' lives, when a mechanical failure caused his plane to crash. *Five Minutes to Impact* is a riveting account of how David survived a traumatic event and emerged with a life-changing message. You will be inspired and challenged by his story.

—KEN R. CANFIELD, PhD
Author, International Speaker, Founder: National Center for Fathering and the National Association for Grand Parenting

It's one thing to be gripped by a "nail-biting" true life story you've never heard. It's another to have heard the story and still be glued to the book to the very end. David Osborne's story is truly one of divine intervention and genuine faith!

—ROSIE J. WILLIAMS
Author of *Repurposed Faith*, Contributing Author to *Military Families Devotional Bible, Faith Deployed Again,* and *Military Wives NT, Psalms and Proverbs*

The most important moment you and I will ever reach in life is the moment when we realize the question of our eternal destiny. On a dark, cloudy night in August of 2012, Dave Osborne was at peace, even in the face of almost certain death. This ordeal inspired Dave's thoughtful contemplation. He shares, "We don't have to live in fear of the present or the future. That was never God's plan for our life." In *Five Minutes to Impact*, Dave shares some of the extraordinary life lessons learned through this ordeal from his perspective as a businessman, father, pilot, and man of faith.

—LONNIE BERGER
Author and President of Every Man a Warrior

You will stop breathing. Your heart will race. You will whisper, "Dear God, no!" *Five Minutes to Impact* is every traveler's nightmare, yet simultaneously an inspiring story of supernatural peace in the darkest hour.

—JIM CONGDON, TH.D
Sr. Pastor Topeka Bible Church, Author, Chairman of Jews for Jesus

FIVE
MINUTES
to
IMPACT

The Final Flight of the Comanche

DAVID F. OSBORNE

AMBASSADOR INTERNATIONAL
GREENVILLE, SOUTH CAROLINA & BELFAST, NORTHERN IRELAND
www.ambassador-international.com

Five Minutes to Impact

The Final Flight of the Comanche

Unless otherwise indicated, Scripture taken from The ESV® Bible (The Holy Bible, English Standard Version®). ESV® Permanent Text Edition® (2016). Copyright © 2001 by Crossway, a publishing ministry of Good News Publishers. The ESV® text has been reproduced in cooperation with and by permission of Good News Publishers. Unauthorized reproduction of this publication is prohibited. All rights reserved.

Scripture marked NIV taken from THE HOLY BIBLE, NEW INTERNATIONAL VERSION®, NIV® Copyright © 1973, 1978, 1984, 2011 by Biblica, Inc.® Used by permission. All rights reserved worldwide.

Scripture marked RSV taken from the Revised Standard Version of the Bible, Copyright © 1946, 1952, and 1971 the Division of Christian Education of the National Council of the Churches of Christ in the United States of America. Used by permission. All rights reserved.

ISBN: 978-1-62020-587-7
eISBN: 978-1-62020-664-5

Page Layout by Hannah Nichols
Ebook Conversion by Anna Riebe Raats

AMBASSADOR INTERNATIONAL
Emerald House
411 University Ridge, Suite B14
Greenville, SC 29601, USA
www.ambassador-international.com

AMBASSADOR BOOKS
The Mount
2 Woodstock Link
Belfast, BT6 8DD, Northern Ireland, UK
www.ambassadormedia.co.uk

The colophon is a trademark of Ambassador

To my wonderful wife, Suzanne, and our children: Daniel, Matthew, Stephen, Kathryn, Jonathan, Carrie, Ruth, Andrew, Tim, their wonderful spouses, and our growing number of grandchildren.

In the course of life and God's timing, may you understand that He is the One that establishes the time of our birth, and the length of our days, that we might grow to understand His providence in the affairs of our short lives.

—Psalm 139

CONTENTS

Part I
MY STORY

Part II

FOR THOSE SEARCHING FOR ANSWERS TO THE DIFFICULT QUESTIONS OF LIFE AND CIRCUMSTANCE

FOREWORD

A TICK OF THE CLOCK, a few seconds of time: without warning, in a moment, everything in life can change. Relying only on a lifetime of preparation, we must navigate that moment. Sometimes, the moment lasts for minutes. Training and reactions take over, accompanied by a torrent of thoughts of eternity and fear of reality. This is what Dave Osborne faced on the night of August 16, 2012. Without warning, his Comanche 260 experienced catastrophic engine failure, transforming the airplane from a wounded, marginally-controllable airship to an unguided missile landing in total darkness, on a road only divine guidance could have found.

The toll of such a near-death experience cannot be fully described. Its aftereffects are sobering. The short-term and long-term emotional and spiritual impacts can only be navigated by the grace of God.

Our friendship with David and Suzanne spans decades; it was cemented by the rescue of our twenty-three-year-old son and teenage daughter from a Kansas blizzard. After receiving a desperate call from my son, I wracked by brain for someone to help them. We had met the Osbornes briefly at a Navigator conference. I remembered that they lived in Kansas, but I was not sure if they were near our stranded kids. I found their phone number, reaching Dave at home on that snowy night. Dave immediately set out to find them and took them into their home. This began a lifelong friendship centered on family, work, flying, and discipleship.

In Dave's story you will see his passion for flying and his commitment to God. You will see his personality—determined, self-reliant, and disciplined. You will see fear and faith, as well as his deep concern for his passengers and his family.

As I read Dave's account of what happened after the accident, I was reminded of another crash in 1988. I had arranged for Air Force security policemen under my responsibility at Hanscom AFB, MA, to be deployed on special duty for security at the 1988 Ramstein AFB Flugfest88 in Germany. On August 28, 1988, three Italian air demonstration fighters collided, crashing and burning right in front of the crowds, killing over seventy and injuring 368. The *Air Force Times* and many newspapers carried a photo of four AF Security Police carrying a victim. These were my security policemen from Hanscom AFB. Many were older, experienced police officers and state patrolmen, police sergeants, and seasoned trauma experts. They saved the lives of many. We immediately brought them home. All were in shock. All were offered counseling to process what had happened and what they had seen and participated in. None of them were injured—a miracle.

Similarly, Dave and his passengers and family had to process this near-death experience emotionally—and especially spiritually. Read on to see how both flight, spiritual training, and the unseen hand of God, saved their lives.

—Dr. Jerry E. White
Major General, USAF, Retired
International President Emeritus, The Navigators
2016, Colorado Springs

ACKNOWLEDGMENTS

My original intent was to have the content of this book be much longer and to cover many more issues than are expressed in the following pages. Others have encouraged me to stay closer to the storyline of an unexpected event late one August evening that would forever change the way I looked at life and my future. From time to time, many of us have experienced events that, statistically, should have produced a different result. In my case, life and death weighed in the balance. My hope is that this story of my life and experience will be interesting to the reader but also encouraging in your journey through life and the pursuit of a lasting purpose.

I am indebted deeply to many people that have helped me through the process of recovery, moving forward, and writing down my story. My wife of forty years has never ceased to encourage me, standing faithfully with me in life's challenges and joys. Through this project, she has spent hours helping work through the details of this book. She is my sounding board, encourager, and the mother of our nine children.

I also want to thank my good friend Dr. Ken Canfield for initially helping motivate me to take on this project. I am indebted to my long-time friend and college roommate, Eric Nordgren, for taking time to read the script and suggest changes in the content and direction. My daughter Carrie helped sort through some of the earlier notes and script, cleaning up the content. I am grateful to our dear family friend Tammy Powell for extensive help in editing the book and checking my grammar. I need to also mention my friend Dr. Jim Congdon, who has been the pastor of a Midwestern church for over forty years now. I am equally grateful for my good friend since college days, Lauren Libby, President/CEO of

Trans World Radio, for taking time from his busy schedule to read the manuscript, encouraging me to finish, and making suggestions to the script. Thank you to Rosie Williams, who encouraged me not to give up when dealing with the challenges of a new experience. And thank you to Katie Smith who, through the publisher, kept the grammar and editing in line with modern rules and to Sam Lowry and his wonderful staff at Ambassador International for being willing to publish this for me.

Lastly, there have been dozens of close friends who I know from our church, the community, work, and civic organizations through the years that have written notes and given words of encouragement through this process. To name them all would be almost impossible, but their concern and help is truly humbling and heartening.

INTRODUCTION

THIS IS MY STORY—AN AVERAGE American growing up in the Midwest during the turbulent 1960s who developed a growing love for aviation. It is a story about an event that has forever changed my outlook and increased my gratefulness for the many privileges we have in this short life. There are no wasted experiences in life when we reflect on them and allow ourselves to learn from them. One late August night, the realization of how fragile and unpredictable the events of life are became unspeakably clear.

This book is written with the express hope that the story will capture the interest of readers. More importantly, it is written with the aspiration that all of us will invest our lives in the things that are permanent and of lasting importance. With those thoughts, my hope is that this will be interesting, entertaining, and life-changing.

Part I

MY STORY

Turning to final approach for landing

Runway 13 at Phillip Billard Airport, looking southeast

CHAPTER 1:

FROM SERENITY TO THE FACE OF DEATH

FROM OUR LAST STOP, WE had traveled just over 300 nautical miles heading for our home base in the heartland of Kansas. It was shortly before 10:00 p.m., and the long days of late summer had finally surrendered to the darkness of night. Since leaving South Dakota almost two hours earlier, the air had become even and still, providing an uneventful flight for my two passengers and myself.

In a little over ten minutes, we would be landing in the warm moonless night at Philip Billard Airport in Topeka, Kansas, bearing the call letters KTOP. The plane would be back in its hangar, my employees and I would be driving home, and we would all be returning to the routine life we were familiar with. The events of that day would soon pass into the distant corners of our minds.

As we soared smoothly through the sky, I looked out the window into the blackness of night that had now completely enveloped us. Moments before, the sky had been clear, but now we were below the overcast above, and the air had become dense from the heavy moisture that had formed as the summer air began to cool. My thoughts began shifting toward home and being reunited with my family. Then, as I had undertaken thousands of times before, I subconsciously began working through the steps in preparation for landing. Everything seemed ordinary and routine.

Due to the calmness of the night, as I began our final descent for Billard Airport, I increased our descent from the normal 500 feet per minute to 700 feet per minute. This would result in increased air and ground speed but keep us in the yellow arc of the airspeed indicator allowable in calm conditions and bring us to the desired airport traffic pattern altitude just north of Topeka.

The euphoric tranquility of life's most serene moments often leaves us unsuspecting of life's most terrifying moments about to unfold. At the time, we had little comprehension of how true that statement could really be. In a moment, we would find out.

Unexpectedly, our senses came to life with a startled jolt. Instantly, the propeller produced a deep, fluttering sound at the distinct loss of power. There was a sensation of falling. The engine began to strain and run rough. Unknowingly, this flash in time would be forever immutably seared deep in the inner reaches of our memories. For a moment, I felt flushed and in shock. Like lightning, adrenaline shot into my system. After that, things seemed to go into slow motion.

Steve and Paul[1], my passengers and employees, were undoubtedly having similar feelings. Although no words were spoken, the silence was piercing. The unnatural roar of the propeller became immediately deafening. The violent banging and shaking of the aircraft intensified quickly as it instantly brought me back to reality; the engine was now obviously beginning to falter.

Instinctively, I pulled back on the control yoke to control the speed of our descent. Our speed was quickly dropping. Our descent was slowed only momentarily. The plane's controls were becoming sluggish and unnatural to me as they vibrated in my hand.

The instruments and gauges that had been perfectly normal only moments before now foreshadowed fatal disaster for the previously-reliable aircraft. The noise and fierce tremors of the plane were forceful and unrelenting. Like a wild animal fighting to save its last breath, the noise only intensified. Our initial shock turned to fear.

As the stark reality of our situation was now indisputable, no one spoke a word, but the realization of what we faced overwhelmed us. In the back seat, Paul, a non-pilot with limited experience in a plane, was no

---

1   Names in this book have been changed to protect the individuals' privacy.

doubt in shock from what was happening around him. He quickly sent a text to his wife to tell her he loved her and to pray for him. Thoughts flooded his mind that this might be his last communication. Slipping the cell phone in his back pocket, hoping to hold onto it if he was thrown from the plane, he remained in silent disbelief as we continued to fall from the sky.

Steve, who had earned a pilot's license a few years prior to this while working at the company, was on my right side in the co-pilot's seat. Wanting to help but at the same time not wanting to distract me, he made minor adjustments to the radio but remained silent. He knew all too well that this was no time for idle conversation. Precious moments of life seemed to be ticking away, slipping from our grasp.

In an instant, my tranquil demeanor had changed. My senses were on full alert, giving razor sharp attention to the plane and our surroundings. Shock and disbelief gripped me as a sudden, precipitous, rushing wind overcame us. I struggled to grasp just what was happening. Our expectations for that evening and the future had been radically altered beyond our control. Along with the sense of helplessness and grim awareness, the seriousness of what we were facing in the lonely darkness of night was beginning to sink in. No one dared utter their thoughts, but the pugnacious reality of what was happening gripped us. We all knew that in a few short moments we were going to die.

Overland Park, Kansas: growing up and 60 years later

CHAPTER 2:

GROWING UP IN KANSAS

I WAS BORN IN THE Kansas City area in 1954. The only child of Harold and Geraldine E. Osborne, our home was in Overland Park while it was still a young and developing community. I have only a few memories of my very early years, but, for the most part, the ones I do have are good ones. I remember that our home on Riley Street had white siding and a finished two-story attic room; they seemed huge to my young eyes, but by today's standards, they would be considered average. Standards, lifestyles, and expectations have changed dramatically in America since that time, but through my adolescence, I was never in need and never knew the difference between how I was raised and those who had much more materially.

I grew up as part of the demographic that would later become known as the "baby boomers." Life could be challenging during this time period. There wasn't an excess of money. Individuals worked hard and tried to save what they could. Church on Sunday was a main event in the week—as it was for most families in those days. Weekly Boy Scout meetings in the city held equal priority. Beyond these events and our small black and white TV, we dreamed large and thought about what we would do or who we would become in the future.

Unfortunately, my parents divorced when I was seven, and I became an unwilling victim of what plagues over half of our population today. My world had changed. I now had a working mother and a strained connection with my father, resulting in little to no relationship with him until I was an adult.

Since my grandparents, Herbert and Laverne Ford, lived only two blocks away, I was fortunate to be able to move in with them. My mother went to work and lived close, but it never seemed like home, and my time was split between locations. My grandparents became an integral part of my life and provided a calm, safe refuge and steady home life for me for the next decade. They were a shelter from the turbulence of my earlier home life. Although I never fully understood its significance until I was older, my grandmother, especially, introduced me to the reality of the presence of God in our world and in my life.

Growing up, there was never a question about whether or not I belonged in their home. When I was older, I always knew their door was open. There would be a meal waiting and, usually, a freshly baked pie. I had a room and a bed that was made and ready for me. It was my home, and I knew they loved me, no matter what. This was much more than many ever had.

Although my life was peaceful and happy with my grandparents, there was something missing in my life that caused restlessness. There was a distance from my father that continued to haunt me into adulthood. My grandfather stepped in as the mentor I needed. He was elderly, and there was a large age gap between us, but he did the best he could. However, the nagging feeling continued, so I searched for what could meet that inner need.

For years, I searched for something or someone to bring real fulfillment and peace to fill the emptiness I felt in my life. Although we attended church on Sundays and I was an active member of the church youth group, religious discussions were never a part of everyday conversations. However, my grandmother regularly read stories from the Bible to me and helped me memorize Psalm 23 and John 3:16. These became pillars of strength and direction throughout my youth and into my adult years. Through this, my grandmother offered the foundation for the deep healing I needed, and later, I eventually found peace in a relationship with God.

During the late summer before my senior year of high school, a friend talked me into joining him at a local youth house, which I later discovered was a youth ministry outreach. I'll never forget Rich Beach, the director of the program, who later became my good friend and mentor. That first night, he discussed things in a way that not only made logical sense, but also reached me internally, overwhelming me with emotion. Was this the missing link that I, and so many others I knew, had been looking for?

I knew God existed from going to church, but until that moment during Rich's talk, I never understood that the God I had heard about was a personal, living Being, who wanted a relationship with me. Something changed in my heart and in my understanding of the purpose of life. I finally understood that my heavenly Father wished to fill the gaps I felt from my biological father's absence. The restless desire to find what was missing in my life was finally replaced with God's love and presence. I finally felt satisfied and at peace.

Since then, my faith has been a central part of my life story; and, although many other defining moments have occurred in my lifetime, it was again tested like never before that August night over the plains of Kansas. This time I would have to trust Him in a way I had never experienced. No matter how hard I wanted things to change that dark night in August, there was no hope in any effort I would make.

Aeronca Champion

Cessna 195

*Kansas has always had a rich aviation history, but during my grandparents'
generation, aviation was in its infancy. My maternal grandmother was born
the year before the Wright brothers made their historic flight at Kitty Hawk.*

CHAPTER 3:

SEEDS OF A PASSION

AS A PILOT, BEFORE THE days of government-issued pilot's licenses, my great-uncle Robert R. Osborne told passionate stories of learning to fly an open cockpit plane in the 1920s by taxiing up and down a grass pasture a few times before hearing the words, "Do you think you have it now?" I wish I would have asked him what the plane was, but just the same, his aviation experience was interesting and thrilling, yet short. While his flying experience fortunately did not end fatally, many in that era did not live long enough to say the same.

Nevertheless, those pioneers of flight with their entrepreneurial spirit shaped the world of aviation and the America I grew up in. From the Wright brothers' first flight to the golden years of aviation to the complex systems of today, aviation grew rapidly, and Orville Wright lived to see Chuck Yeager, whom I met a few years ago, break the sound barrier in 1947. Today, aviation has become one of the statistically safest forms of travel.

As a young person, I always had a fascination with airplanes. For hours, I worked on building plastic models of various planes—normally WWII vintage. Some of those models I built several times, always trying to improve on the next one. From an early age, I was always somewhat of a perfectionist. If I glued something in the wrong place, I was never satisfied. I would stay awake into the late hours of night to work on my models and read about the planes I was building.

My uncle, Herbert H. Ford, Jr., was my mother's only brother. He, too, had grown up with a love of aviation. Herb took a special interest in me, and we always got along well. Herb was a member of the EAA (Experimental

Aircraft Association) and, for years, was the chapter president in Kansas City. It was during that time that he rebuilt an Aeronca Champion, affectionately referred to, by him, as "Tweety Bird." The Aeronca Champion was first introduced to the public in 1945 and was often just referred to as a "Champ." It was a single engine, tandem, two-seat plane with a fixed main landing gear and a tail wheel in the back (called a "tail dragger").

First built and flown in 1944, the military would later enlist some of these Aeronca Champs, changing the name to L-16's. With an imposing cruising speed of only about eighty-five miles per hour, they would not set any speed records. Nevertheless, they would still be used for a variety of services including lightweight delivery, reconnaissance, and passenger transport.

Later on, Herb also acquired a Cessna 195. The 195 was also a "tail dragger" airplane, but much larger. Built between 1947 and 1954, they were powered by radial engines and could seat up to five people. Due to the tail wheel landing gear configuration, landings could be tricky. Takeoffs were not much better; there was limited forward visibility because the nose was up in the air until the plane was airborne.

Herb never earned an instrument rating and had no interest in flying at night or even in remotely adverse conditions. He was a cautious pilot that considered a puff of cloud in the distance as instrument conditions. Nevertheless, he was an excellent pilot, and in 1970, he took me on my first flight in a private airplane. That flight lit the flame to an already growing interest in aviation that continues to this day.

CHAPTER 4:

THE FIRST FLIGHT

GROWING UP, MY LOVE OF aviation grew only stronger with time. It was late in my high school days that my uncle took me on my first single engine flight in a PT-19 early WWII trainer. This day's flight would be from Johnson County Executive Airport, known by its FAA identifier as KOJC located in Olathe, Kansas.

I was thrilled to go that summer afternoon, so off we went. The old mono wing trainer was painted in navy blue and yellow (similar to the stock photo above). It had a small engine with minimal instrumentation or frills. However, there were enough instruments to make it legal; it was easy to fly; and we were free as a bird to go where we wanted. The one difficulty was its narrow wheelbase that could make it easy to ground loop.

For those who don't know what a ground loop is—early aircraft had a tail wheel in the back, and the landings were quite different from the tricycle gear commonly used today where the nose wheel is in the front. Tail draggers, as they are referred to, are a little like driving a car at high speeds in reverse; but since the center of gravity is behind the wheels, it wants to move the back end to the front on landings, which has made for a bad day with many a pilot. It isn't hard to get a rapid spin in the horizontal plane when the back of the plane thinks it wants to be where the front is. At the very least, this could be embarrassing to a young pilot and, in many cases, proved dangerous and damaging to the plane and passengers.

Nevertheless, there wasn't that much to it, and it had earned the name by some as the "Cradle of Heroes," having been one of the early primary trainers for many men flying in the military. To me, despite its simplicity, it was beautiful. I could envision heroes and young men scarcely older than I who had trained in this plane or one similar. Many had gone to war, some had returned, and many had not, but they had given us our freedom, and I was experiencing a piece of their history.

Sporting its rudimentary instruments, the plane glided through the air with ease as we listened to the defining but distinctive chugging of the old inline engine still serving the designer's purpose. As we flew over those farm fields of Kansas, my uncle gave me the stick with some basic instruction on how the foot pedals worked the rudder and how they needed to be coordinated together. Our form of communication in those days was by talking back and forth through an air tube attached to a leather helmet.

Strapped in by a six-point harness, steep turns or loops could be somewhat nerve-racking when you realized that the only thing between you and the ground were those straps over your shoulders and lap, along with whatever they might be fastened to. The view, however, was exhilarating. I could see the homes below, the barns, the roads, the rolling hills, and the greenish-brown hues of late summer. We never flew too high, so the visibility was perfect for looking out in all directions, except straight down. It was a summer day, and the pale blue sky filled with moisture, added to the laid-back feeling of summer.

The enthralling freedom of the experience could easily bring an intoxicating affixation with flight—as it did for me. Below, where we lived, were the joys and pains of life, but now we were above all of that as I felt God must have wanted us to live. That moment would forever seal my love for and lifetime involvement in aviation. All my childhood dreams finally came together that day, and I was forever hooked.

My youth was quickly passing, and my college years were soon approaching. I had the privilege of attending Kansas State University in Manhattan and later earned an engineering degree. It was during that first year that my mother passed away, followed by my grandfather later the same year. Again, my life had changed. At eighteen, I really felt like I was on my own.

A few opportunities for flying came and went, and I never lost a love or interest in aviation. However, many years passed before time, money, and circumstance would allow me to complete my own license.

Flying never left my thoughts for long. The independence and freedom that flying brings not only provided me with joy, relaxation, and fulfillment, but also came to serve business and financial purposes later in life. It became an essential part of my business growth and ability to provide for a family. One day, it also brought me to the edge of death, but for now, I was thrilled to have had my first flight.

Flying a Cherokee-6 off of Manhattan Regional Airport with my wife, Suzanne, and two oldest boys, Daniel and Matthew.

CHAPTER 5:

A PRIVATE PILOT

IT WAS DURING THOSE COLLEGE years that I met my future wife, Suzanne, over Christmas break in 1972. For me, it was love at first sight. I never dated or had an interest in any other girl after that time. We saw each other occasionally throughout the year and more often during holidays and summer breaks. We stayed in touch through handwritten letters, a form of communication now incomprehensible to our children. On August 1, 1976, we were finally married.

Although I never lost my desire to pursue flying, my goals of flying and additional college degrees were not conducive with my fledgling business and children that began to come at a seemingly ever-increasing rate. I could never seem to squeeze out the time or money to continue my sky-high passion. Nonetheless, attaining my pilot's license never left my mind.

After years of determination, I finally earned my own private pilot's license in 1985 at the Manhattan, Kansas, airport, known by FAA identifier KMHK. Although I usually flew a Cessna 172, Piper Archer, or something similar, I flew whatever I could get my hands on as money and time would allow. To date, there are several dozen types of aircraft I have had the privilege of flying. Whenever I had a project in Kansas City or somewhere that had an airport, I chose to fly, even though the entire process took just as long as driving.

When the kids were still young, I would pack them two deep into the back seat of a Cessna 172, and off we would go. Usually, we were right at, or close to, the gross maximum weight allowed in the aircraft. Therefore, a slow ascent to altitude was common. Invariably, once we were finally at altitude, someone would need to use a bathroom. No amount of threatening, pleading, or patience changed the situation, and creativity is often spurred on by necessity. I think it is safe to say that there were a few baby bottles that never got used again for feeding; and from that standpoint, we were lucky to have mostly boys. The biggest problem was who held the bottle; and, if we hit an air pocket, things went from bad to worse in a hurry.

Fortunately, most of the kids never minded flying, except my oldest son. Prone to motion sickness, his stomach almost always became upset. This even escalated to the point that he would throw up before the flight. When asked if he wasn't feeling well before one flight, he simply replied, "I'm getting over it ahead of time." On the contrary, my second son, now a Blackhawk pilot with the Kansas Army National Guard, would stand up in the back and shout "Whee! This is fun, just like a roller coaster!" Nothing daunted his exuberance, even during some major turbulence, when we flew near a tornado in Hot Springs, Arkansas, one spring day. After a quick landing, my wife kissed the ground, but Matthew simply said, "That was fun. What are we doing now, Dad?"

Since a bigger and faster aircraft is the dream of almost any pilot, I was constantly looking for opportunities to fly such a plane. I was able to fly a Mooney M-20, which helped fulfill some of that dream. Its slick aerodynamic body sliced through the sky, but it was still only a four-seat airplane, limited in weight capacity, but, most of all, limited in size, since I am a big guy.

Later on, some friends offered me flying privileges in a six-seat Piper Cherokee Six. Although not as fast as the Mooney, it could haul anything that you could fit through the door. Soon after, the same friends purchased a Piper Saratoga. This plane had the same fuselage but a bigger engine, retractable gear, carrying capacity of a six-seat airplane, and a large side door with club seating in the back. It was an easy airplane for me to fly, and it was much more comfortable with any added weight and its extra capacity.

In 1992, I finally obtained my instrument rating. Since then, I have flown many types of airplanes, both single and twin-engine, logging several thousand hours. However, the Comanche came to be my main aircraft about ten years later, receiving approximately 75 percent of my flight time during that period of time. It proved to be an economical and stable airplane with great fuel and carrying capacity. Little did I know that my passion for flight and this airplane would one day lead me to the brink of eternity.

The North Dakota oil industry was expanding at an exponential rate during our trip in 2012.

CHAPTER 6:

KANSAS TO NORTH DAKOTA

IT WAS MID-AUGUST, AND THE sultry days of summer were common on the Kansas prairie at that time of year. Those days are often referred to as the "dog days of summer" because of the euphoric feeling they can bring.

It was easy to have a relaxed feeling during the final day that I would fly my plane. Reflecting on the events of summer, this would come to an end all too soon. Vacations would be over, the younger generation would be heading back to school, and for some, college life would resume. This was true for several of my own children who were still in high school and college. However, for most of us, it meant we were back to the normal routines of life, work, and family, with the joys and challenges they bring. For now, however, those thoughts remained distant as we basked in the waning day's antecedent of late summer and early fall.

The humid temperatures were still reaching the mid 80-degree level back home in Topeka, Kansas. However, the weather patterns had not yet changed, and the warm summer air brought long periods of high pressure with generally clear skies. This day, the normally dark blue skies were softened by the higher humidity that often comes that time of year. This made the weather for flying small aircraft under "Visual Flight Rules" about as close to perfect as it gets.

"Visual Flight Rules" are specific guidelines set up by the Federal Aviation Administration that establish the procedures a pilot must follow when the weather is clear enough that he or she can safely navigate visually without the sole use of instruments.

Consequently, my business flight plan from Topeka to North Dakota would be a long but easy, uneventful flight.

On Wednesday morning, August 15, 2012, Steve, Paul, and I climbed into our high-performance, complex-rated, Piper Comanche 260 R airplane for our trip to North Dakota, where we planned to check on several projects and job sites. Although the Comanche airplane was old (originally made in 1964), one would never know by its appearance. Few original moving parts remained, and the cockpit instruments had given way to the new digital age, including navigational NEXRAD radar that would download and update itself every few minutes. This made the plane a dream to fly and navigate for a small time private pilot.

The 260 HP-rated, fuel injection of the Lycoming IO-540 engine made the Comanche what the FAA considered "high performance." The retractable landing gear, the adjustable landing flaps, and the movable propeller blades to keep the RPM constant in flight gave it a "complex" rating as well. The relatively new paint on the exterior was deceptive to all but experienced aviators, and it was not uncommon to receive compliments from fellow pilots flying similar class airplanes. We were far from being in the same league with the corporate jets, but for us, it served our purposes well. It was economical and a plane I could easily handle without a copilot.

Steve had worked for the company for several years. He had served in several roles, but at this time was working with clients managing projects we were constructing. Since many of our projects were out of state, Steve had earned his private pilot's license as well, which was helpful when visiting distant locations when the weather allowed. Furthermore, the presence of a second pilot always helps to assist with the flight's workload and breaks the boredom of long distances. Consequently, Steve was in the right seat next to me during the flight to and from North Dakota.

Paul, hired three days prior, also traveled with us. Although Paul did not have a vast background in construction, he was immediately available, was familiar with the North Dakota area, and seemed to be a good fit for our short-term position to help keep an eye on the progress of the job sites.

Our flight from Philip Billard Airfield to our destination of Tioga, North Dakota, took about four and a half hours. We enjoyed our time together, visiting and viewing the earth below with its ever-changing terrain. Although ultimately uneventful, it was a long trip with a slight head wind. However, with a brief stop halfway in Paschal, South Dakota, for fuel and to stretch, the time passed quickly. I have loved flying since my teenage years, and, although age had brought moderation to the thrill and exhilaration, I still had not lost the love of crawling in the cockpit and the freedom that flying brings.

Business was conducted uneventfully in Tioga. Our two commercial projects were about to be completed, and we had managed to meet with all of the needed subcontractors and foremen for the jobs. Soon enough, we were once again at the small airport in Tioga, ready to depart.

NEW TOWN MUNI (Ø5D)   1 SE   UTC–6(–5DT)   N47°58.07′ W102°28.69′

1923   NOTAM FILE GFK
RWY 12–30: H3420X60 (ASPH)   S–5   MIRL
  RWY 12: PAPI(P2L). Tank.
  RWY 30: PAPI(P2L). Road.
SERVICE: **LGT** ACTIVATE MIRL Rwy 12–30—CTAF.
AIRPORT REMARKS: Unattended. Deer on or invof arpt. Birds invof arpt near
  lagoon. Rwy 12–30 snow removal irregular, for rwy condition call
  701–627–4722/701–627–4717 or 701–898–4918.
AIRPORT MANAGER: (701) 898-4918
COMMUNICATIONS: CTAF 122.9
RADIO AIDS TO NAVIGATION: NOTAM FILE ISN.
  WILLISTON (L) VORW/DME 116.3   ISN   Chan 110   N48°15.21′
  W103°45.04′   096° 54.0 NM to fld. 2372/12E.   **HIWAS.**

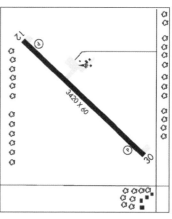

New Town, North Dakota Airport

CHAPTER 7:

TIOGA, NEW TOWN, AND MITCHELL, SOUTH DAKOTA

IT WAS THURSDAY MORNING ON the 16th of August that Steve, Paul, and I were looking forward to a flight back home from Tioga, North Dakota. After a cup of coffee and some less than satisfactory hotel food, we headed for the unmanned Tioga airport. Reminiscent of the rapidly diminishing frontier airports, we called the number on the gas pumps for assistance. About fifteen minutes later, someone arrived and our main and auxiliary tanks were filled with fuel from the remote little airport's fuel tank. The Comanche had been equipped with almost every speed modification and upgrade the FAA would allow, and one of those upgrades was the installation of wing tip tanks, in addition to the main and auxiliary tanks found in each wing.

 With inboard main fuel tanks, auxiliary fuel tanks, and wing tip tanks, the plane would hold 120 gallons of fuel, which was enough to fly as much as six to eight hours at a reasonable altitude. Although this is longer than almost anyone ever wants to sit at one time, it was a nice safety factor. As Steve Stutzman fueled the plane, I rested in the airport building, often referred to as the "Pilot's Shack," for a few minutes, collecting my thoughts on what the day would bring and what we needed to accomplish.

There was a nice gentleman, probably about my age, who was a commercial pilot waiting for his passengers. We struck up a conversation for a few minutes but never exchanged last names. I remember he was Tom and had been in and out of that airport a number of times. If we meet again, we will no doubt have plenty to discuss about our very different flights home. After fueling, I checked the plane one last time, and after boarding, went through our normal pre-departure checklist. We then headed off for a short flight to New Town, South Dakota, where one of our smaller projects would soon begin.

Tioga's airport had a modern runway in good condition, however, New Town was another story. Although safe for us, the runway was only 3000 feet long and fifty feet wide. In deteriorating condition, it would accommodate only a light twin at best, and there were no services at all, including fuel. Similar to many small airports in remote parts of the country, there was a lonely trailer where transient pilots could get in out of the weather or wait out a storm. Inside, hanging on the wall, the keys to a courtesy car could be found for those needing a ride to town.

Most private airports rely on the generosity and camaraderie of the local fellow pilots. Therefore, courtesy vehicles, as well as any other airport services, are usually donated, and one never knows what might be available to them. The vehicle at this particular airport proved to be a bigger challenge than most as it was filthy, and the power steering didn't work. For all of us who have experienced trying to drive without power steering in a car designed for it, you know it isn't any fun and is not safe. Nevertheless, we made it into town and tried to find some fluid we could add to the steering pump in hopes of an easier return trip.

After our meeting and a quick lunch with various subcontractors, we decided to head home. Even with a light tail wind, it would still entail four hours of flying on our return trip. Therefore, we decided to stop in Mitchell, South Dakota, just over half the return distance. Since it was a good-sized airport, they would have anything that we would need, including fuel and a ride to town for a quick meal.

Once in Mitchell, the weather was again almost perfect as we climbed out of the plane. It was early evening, and the temperature was in the upper seventies with a gentle breeze rolling across the deserted ramp area. The sky was soft blue, accented only by the a few small cumulus clouds that pilots often call "scuds" dotting the sky.

This was the last stop of our almost 1200-mile journey, and as we looked around, the entire airport seemed deserted. As we approached the "fixed base operators" known as the FBO, we remarked how clean and well-groomed the lawn was. It was dark green, thick, and without a weed in sight and was kept in perfect order. The FBO will normally sell fuel, often give flight instruction, and commonly offer maintenance at larger airports.

Unfortunately, the FBO had closed operations for the day only minutes earlier. Steve called the after-hours number to see if there was a possibility of getting some fuel or using the courtesy car. It was my personal habit to buy fuel from any FBO I stopped at since smaller ones were usually struggling and appreciated the support from pilots to stay in business. Furthermore, although we weren't lacking in fuel, I liked to keep my tanks full for emergencies and always avoided cutting it close.

However, the fuel attendant Steve called had no intention of returning to fuel a small aircraft. I was never in on the phone conversation, but I remember Steve being mildly irritated that the person on the other end had no interest in helping out a small plane. Trying several tactics from pleading to dogmatism, he finally gave up. Nevertheless, we had plenty of fuel to get home with well over an hour of reserve. This was considered plenty in good weather conditions, so we dismissed further discussion on the subject. Little did we know, this might have been one of several factors that would lead to saving our lives only a few hours later.

We discussed whether to continue home or go into town for dinner. Since we had no pressing schedule, a vote was taken, and we decided to stay. About that time, a classic '70s car, immaculately restored, pulled up to the gate, driven by a teenager heading to the airport for his senior picture. Before long, the young man had pulled out a nice-looking Piper Archer, four-place airplane, the smaller brother of what I was flying, in a perceptible effort to complement the photo shoot.

Steve walked over to him and asked if he knew how we could get to town. I think in the back of his mind a fellow pilot surely wouldn't mind letting us borrow that nice-looking classic Camaro for a few minutes. Instead, he returned only with the name of a taxi service. After a few more minutes of discussion, Steve called a taxi. As twenty minutes passed, the taxi that should have been there in five minutes was still not there. Never having an abundance of patience, I paced the parking lot, even though we weren't on a schedule. When the taxi finally arrived, we simply wanted somewhere quick to go, have dinner, and arrive back at the airport quickly.

The Corn Palace in Mitchell, South Dakota.

After asking what Mitchell was famous for, we found that the "Corn Palace" was one place they were proud of! "Oh well, what is another five minutes?" we commented. "We are here, drive us by it." We all agreed. It was unique with large mosaics of corn on the walls and grass columns. The drought had prevented the replacement of the mosaics for the first time in its history. It was interesting, but not what we came for, and, with interest quickly waning, we headed off to the restaurant. The driver's "quick and back" recommendation for a place to eat was no doubt a good friend, or at least one that gives a meal here or there after referrals. The food was acceptable, but fast food it was not.

By the time we finally returned to the airport and into the airplane, almost two hours had passed. Nightfall was now quickly approaching, and we would no longer be home before dark. Normally, this would not have been a concern or anything out of the ordinary, but tonight would be different.

CHAPTER 8:

MITCHELL, SOUTH DAKOTA TO TOPEKA, KANSAS

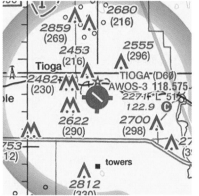

BEING FURTHER NORTH, THE AIR was cool and calm as we went through the pre-flight inspection outside of the plane. Checking the engine oil, we seemed to be in the normal operating range. The Comanche would hold up to seventeen quarts, but normal operating range was around nine. Furthermore, it would still cool and properly lubricate the engine on as little as two and a half quarts. The designers had truly created a phenomenal piece of American engineering; but if it ran without any oil, its life span would be short.

We announced on the CTAF (common traffic

Mitchell, South Dakota, Airport. FAA sectional chart and "fly-in" photograph. Notice the green lawn. We were parked about where the red plane in the center is shown.

advisory frequency) for that airport, that we were taxiing. Heading down the taxiway for departure, we again ran into the father and his young graduate with his cars and airplane now arranged on the taxiway waiting for the perfect sunset as a background to his high school picture. We edged up, but it was apparent that they had no intention of moving. Giving in, we edged our way around, headed back down the taxiway we had come from, and taxied down the runway in the opposite direction (called "back taxiing") to get to our takeoff point.

Before pilots leave the ground and take to the sky, they go through a series of checks pertinent to the airplane they are flying. This is normally referred to as a "run up," since the engine RPM is accelerated. This checks the operation of the magnetos and constant speed propeller, as well as several other aircraft functions and apparatus.

A magneto is part of the ignition system that produces power to the spark plugs. Magnetos are used in airplanes as they are more reliable and less likely to fail than a battery. There are also two magnetos making them a redundant system. Since they send electric impulses to the engine spark plugs, the timing of that spark is as important as it is in a car and even more so in a high-performance aircraft engine. Consequently, if there is any apparent failure, a new magneto is installed, slightly tightened, rotated to the correct timing, and then tightened down to a specific torque setting.

The right magneto in our airplane had been replaced the week prior due to my discovery on an earlier pre-flight that it was not functioning correctly on a "run-up." I had experienced several bad magnetos in my career, and you can check them on the ground by isolating the right and left magnetos separately. Normally, when one magneto (often abbreviated as a "mag") is malfunctioning, there is an obvious drop in RPM, and the engine will run roughly. A check of the mags at 1900 RPM this day did not indicate anything of concern to Steve or me. A fifty to seventy-five RPM drop was normal with the maximum recommended drop being 125. This is something that would later plague our memories as we searched for clues as to what we could have done differently.

During the "run-up" procedure, I cycled the constant speed propeller. The propeller pitch control runs on engine oil through a governor that keeps the RPM relatively constant at various altitudes and power settings. This allows the pilot to turn in a greater angle of attack on the blades during takeoff and landing for maximum thrust or "bite into the air." At the same time, we can reduce the RPM on warm days or when the engine is under excessive load to keep it cool and within normal operating range. As we would later find out, the loss of this control can cause serious problems for a pilot.

After a successful "run-up," we proceeded down the runway for a successful takeoff in a southeast departure route. As we rolled down the runway and lifted off, the Comanche performed perfectly as it had so many times before. We were quickly off the ground, pulled the gear up, and, at 400 feet, we raised the flaps. Flaps are inboard extensions of the trailing edge of the wing lowered to produce more lift at a slower speed on takeoff and landing. I adjusted the manifold pressure to twenty-five inches and the RPM to 2500—what is often referred to as twenty-five squared—and began a slow turn to the south. When we were lined up on course, I activated the Garmin 430 navigation, and our pre-programmed course came up on the screen. Enabling the autopilot, we continued our climb to altitude and were on our way.

Everything seemed to be perfect, but, as we departed, I thought I heard a slight vibration or change in the engine's sound. My good friend Marvin, an experienced pilot, had often told me that I made flight control adjustments by the sound of the airplane. Marvin had taught two of my sons, Matthew and Stephen, how to fly years earlier. I had a lot of respect for his ability and wisdom when it came to flying. I have found this piece of information to be true over the years, and, in addition, I apparently do have acute hearing. It would be a potent reminder in the future that something not sounding quite right gives reason for caution.

However, it was a faint noise and not completely unusual for a single engine to make a few different noises here and there. Even a change in wind direction can sometimes make the prop sound different or flutter. I didn't wish to alarm my passengers by commenting on it, but I didn't want to ignore it either. A thorough scan of the instruments showed nothing to be concerned about as the oil temperature, pressure, suction, throttle, prop, and gas settings all seemed normal. I slightly changed the RPM and manifold pressure to see if anything changed, but just as slight and fast as it came, it had quickly subsided, and the abnormal sound was gone.

My good friend and part owner of the airplane, Jay, has often said jokingly, "An airplane will normally warn you before it kills you." This phrase had always stuck with me and would be yet another foreshadowing of what would happen later that night. Looking back, I continue to wonder if this enigma I had heard was a warning, something totally unrelated, or nothing at all?

We soon leveled off at our altitude of 7500 feet above sea level, and everything was normal. I pressed the rest of the throttle in for maximum manifold pressure, which reduces as the altitude increases. After adjusting the RPM, I then backed off the fuel flow to around fifteen gallons per hour before leaning out the engine to its best fuel usage. It was now time to change from the main tank and burn the remaining fuel from the auxiliary mid wing tanks. The Comanche had six fuel tanks, and keeping track of time burned and fuel flow on each tank can be a daunting task at times.

The flight from Mitchell was uneventful, and we had a pleasant conversation on the way back about a number of subjects. As the conversation lulled, my mind began to shift to thoughts of arriving home to my family. Soon the plane would be on the ground, back in the hangar, and we would be headed home, back to the routine of life we were all accustomed to. The events of that day would soon pass into the distant corners of our minds—or so we assumed.

CHAPTER 9:

THE FINAL DESCENT TO TOPEKA

A night view of Topeka, Kansas, from north

APPROACHING FORTY MILES NORTH OF Topeka, we dialed in the Topeka AWOS (Active Weather Observation Service) into my number two radio. This would give us the local winds and altimeter setting for our correct altitude, as well as the current winds, airport conditions, and any relevant weather. Thirty-seven miles from Topeka, we began our descent. Reaching for the center of the instrument panel, I cranked in two partial turns of the red Vernier fuel mixture knob. This would raise the fuel flow to somewhere around sixteen gallons per hour ensuring that with the thicker air of a lower altitude, the plane's fuel mixture would not run too lean.

I normally preferred a steeper descent at night than the standard 500 FPM (feet per minute) to keep altitude as long as possible, but Paul had already been having trouble with his ears, and I didn't want to cause him any extra discomfort. With this in mind, at about thirty-seven miles from the airport, we began to lose altitude, descending toward Topeka. This would eventually put us close to the airport's pattern altitude a mile or two from home. We could make any last-minute changes we needed when we were closer. In six minutes, we would be landing at the airport. None of us had any idea what the next few minutes would bring and how our lives would be changed forever.

I reached to the ceiling and made a turn on the trim. This adjusts a small tab at the rear of the airplane's horizontal stabilizer, which helps obtain the wanted pitch and speed without excessive pressure on the control yoke. Lowering the manifold pressure, the engine throttled back and slowed slightly. I eased off holding back pressure on the yoke, since I had reduced engine power, and the nose dropped slightly. The plane pitched over gently, and we began to lose altitude. We had over 170 knots of airspeed on the Garmin 430 GPS, which indicated just less than 200 MPH across the ground.

With a gentle tailwind, we had picked up speed with our descent. The air was heavy with moisture, and I could just barely make out what I thought might be the faint glow of Topeka on the horizon ahead of us. The small town of Holton was closer to the east of us and was more visible as the yellow and golden glow of Holton's street lights, parking lights, and civilization pierced lazily through the haze. It was only slightly more visible than the faint illumination of Topeka on the horizon ahead.

As we were now closer to home, the sky had become overcast; the moon behind the clouds was completely dark, and I would later find out that it had less than one percent of visible reflection that night, providing no stars for reference or illumination. With the overcast sky and heavy moisture in the air, it had become completely black. A glance outside revealed only the faint illumination of yard lights peppering the earth below with a black, velvety haze filling the humid sky. As often happens in the summer, the hot air filled with moisture mixed with the cool air of evening. A gentle fog blanketed the ground, obscuring the ground and blurring the lights trying to break through.

The serene feeling of floating past the city lights to the east and the darkness of night below soon left my mind as I returned my focus to the plane, where I would begin a landing checklist. Once again scanning my instruments, everything was normal. I had recently cycled through the EGT (engine gas temperature) gauge, which also indicated the CHT (cylinder head temperature) and oil temperature. The CHT and oil temperature were not primary instruments, so these were checked only periodically, while the other primary instruments were scanned every few seconds.

My normal routine was to check on fuel tank changes about every fifteen minutes. The Comanche had only a few moving parts that were original as most had been replaced through the years. The oil pressure gauge and oil temperature gauges were old needle gauges to the far right of the instrument panel—similar to what you would have seen in a car of that vintage. It was one of the few, if not only, instruments that had not been changed. I despised those gauges because they were hard to read in the daylight and poorly illuminated at night.

The oil temperature gauge was similar to what you would find in a car, so I made a habit of checking the digital version on the EGT gauge on a regular basis. Although that was part of my normal engine instrument scan, it will remain a mystery, plaguing me, whether it had dropped earlier in the flight, and I had not noticed it as we prepared to land. We were now in a steady descent for Topeka that would be the plane's last.

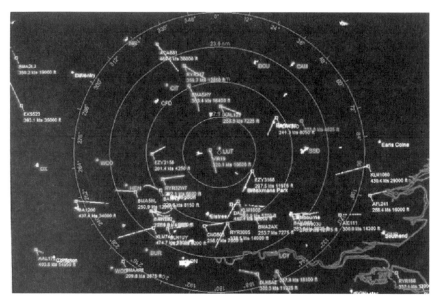

*A typical radar screen similar to the one the controller at Kansas City
Center would have been watching while tracking my movement, location,
and altitude.*

CHAPTER 10:

INCONCEIVABLE DENIAL

ONLY A MINUTE HAD PASSED since we had begun starting down in preparation for landing. Suddenly, something neither pilot nor passenger ever wants to experience began to unfold before our unsuspecting eyes. When we had least expected it, the tranquility of night on the journey's final leg changed in an instant.

Without warning, the lulling hum of the engine had changed to a loud, howling roar. Unusual sounds and vibrations assaulted our senses. The propeller changed pitch angle, fluttered back and forth for a second in time, and then gave way to a high-pitched, growling, whirring sound. Instantly, I could feel the loss of thrust as the large, three-bladed propeller assembly was no longer pulling us through the air.

A strong smell of sulfur gave us the illusion of burning rubber that began to permeate the cabin almost instantaneously. Without hesitation, I made the definitive statement and asked the question in the same breath, "What is that smell?"

As my mind raced for answers, those would be the last words I recall speaking to the passengers that night while we were still in the plane. I questioned myself as my mind went into analytic mode. *Is a belt burning? Are we on fire?* As quickly as those thoughts came, they were dismissed. I knew the Comanche doesn't have belts!

It was definitely an oil smell. There was no hysteria, but adrenaline shot into my system, and my senses snapped to attention like they had been shocked from an electric outlet. Any lethargic acquiescence to the flight being over shortly was no longer met with welcome anticipation.

The propeller was running away at full RPM now. This was faster than I had ever heard or felt the plane reach. The plane began to shake violently, like a wild animal fighting for survival. From that point on, I could never clearly read any of the instruments as the sturdy, old plane developed a relentless vibration. We would only later guess that the three-bladed propellers may have reached speeds of over twice their normal design speed.

In normal flight, every revolution of the propeller by the powerful IO-540 engine would thrust us through over six feet of distance. However, no longer were the proud and sleek, meticulously-designed propeller blades cutting into the air and producing thrust. The fine-tuned precision engine was struggling, and, with the loss of oil pressure, all hydraulic control of the propeller was lost.

Since the engine and propeller share the same oil reservoir, the blades had now retracted from a cutting angle into the wind to a configuration that was flat against our forward motion. The propeller assembly had now become non-aerodynamic and was producing drag as if it were pushing a giant spinning disk through the air.

The controls were stiff, even less responsive, and jerky. This was something you could not practice. It didn't feel the same as when we practiced "engine outs" during training sessions. This impending disaster was the real thing. Only few have lived to tell their story.

I quickly looked to the right at the RPM and manifold gauges, but I couldn't read them clearly. The manifold pressure gauge measures the pressure in the engine, but I could tell it was dropping. The instruments worked perfectly, but the gray-on-gray digital numbers were difficult to read, even in normal daylight hours, and nearly impossible in a smoke-filled cabin with a vibrating instrument panel, so I will never know exactly what was going on in that engine.

A series of green lights line the circumference of the RPM gauge. These were visual indicators of the RPM percentage, and, at this moment, every light shone brightly, in addition to a red LED light at the end, denoting a "too high" over-speed RPM warning. Red lights on an instrument panel are never a good sign and cause tension for passengers. Tonight, every red light was on. All the gauges with needle pointers were vigorously bouncing out of control, and the blurry digital instruments were impossible to read.

My brain went into overdrive as I searched for answers, scanning the instruments and listening to what the plane was trying to tell me. As I began pulling back on the controls to slow our descent, the unthinkable happened. The smoke-filled cockpit and runaway propeller was met with only more noise. The engine was now banging loudly, and I could tell it wasn't going to keep running much longer. It would be the next day before I fully understood why. Less than twenty-four hours later, the FAA would find the block and engine heads perforated from valve stems and piston rods.

I tried adjusting the mixture and manifold throttle pressure, hoping, by some miracle, I might keep the engine going until we could make it home. The engine was running coarsely, and I pressed the remainder of the throttle and fuel mixture in attempting to manage the situation, trying to come to grips with the fact that the engine was about to quit. Nevertheless, I had to try to keep it running. The engine continued to bang and vibrate with increasing ferocity. By now, all hope was quickly vanishing.

FAA Air traffic controllers, similar to Kansas City Center

CHAPTER 11:

GRASPING FOR HELP

BY THIS TIME, THE COCKPIT had completely filled with smoke, and it was becoming difficult to breathe. My mind raced for how I could get fresh air. *Do I open the pilot's window, push open the door, or break out a window with the hand axe behind the passenger seat? Will this extra air accelerate the burning and bring flames into the cockpit? How do I keep from being suffocated before we land?*

I was still processing what was happening—partly in denial and partly in shock of the reality. It had not yet occurred to me that this was burning oil, and there was only so much in the aircraft engine. The next concern was preventing anything else from catching fire or possibly igniting the remaining fuel. While the plane continued to vibrate aggressively, we struggled to breathe the thick, acrid air.

I have heard stories of Comanche pilots landing with their legs on fire, and I never forgot those stories. The fear of fire and asphyxiation were real fears looming over us that night, which only added to the stress of decisions I would soon be forced to make.

Since it had become painfully obvious we were having a problem I could not fix, and the cockpit was full of smoke, staying in the air longer didn't seem wise, especially if there was a fire. After facing the actuality that there were no airports I could reach, I had let the plane continue in a steep descent; and the airspeed picked up, but we weren't speeding to a destination. We were rapidly losing altitude and falling closer and closer to the approaching ground.

I don't think any of us ever were in a state of panic that night; but if I ever came close, it was with the thought that I might not be able to breathe much longer because of the smoke. Consequently, I made the decision to allow our descent to increase in speed.

The hardest thing for any pilot to give up is altitude. As the saying goes for pilots, "The one thing that never does you any good in an emergency is the altitude you have lost." At the same time, a steeper descent might help put out a potential fire and get us to the ground while we could still breathe.

I once again eased off on the control yokes and back pressure. As the nose continued to pitch over, we went into a steep descent, painfully hastening the inevitable. We were now losing altitude more rapidly. It would not be long until we would come in contact with something on the ground. There was no time left for denial.

Over many previous flights, during the long hours of solo and cross-country flight, I had often rehearsed what I would do in case of emergency. I always wanted to know where I could immediately find the nearest airport location. From my standard screen on the Garmin 430, three clicks of the knob to the right would tell me my distance and the degree of radial to the nearest reference point or airport if I had to call an emergency location.

As I automatically reached to turn the GPS locator knob on the vibrating instrument panel, I stopped myself. Although the digital readouts were blurred, I knew we were about 30 miles north of Topeka, and I knew there were no airports that I would reach that night due to my familiarity with the area.

Only a minute had passed but it seemed an eternity. I was rapidly coming to grips with what had happened, and I peered into the darkness for a place to land. Through the years, I have made a habit of always keeping the local FAA controlling center frequency programmed on the radio in second position, even if I wasn't in direct communication or on an Instrument Flight Plan where it would be required. But I hadn't done it for the last leg of this flight; I was coming home, and I knew it by heart. Barely able to read the screen, I quickly dialed in 123.8. I punched the flip button below the frequency, and it jumped to the number one position. My first call for help was at approximately 9:58 p.m.

I called Kansas City Center, which controls air traffic in that area. "Comanche November eight-five-four-six-papa, we've got a possible emergency here; stand by please," I reported.

Comanche 8546P was my call sign, identifier, and the number painted on the side of the airplane. A faint voice returned, "Comanche eight-five-four-six-papa calling Kansas City, say again, someone calling Kansas City," came the reply as we grasped for a glimmer of hope.

CHAPTER 12:

A PETULANT DESCENT

AS I TURNED UP THE volume on my radio, I called Kansas City Center again and repeated as clearly and calmly as possible, "Kansas City Center, Comanche, eight-five-four-six-papa, with possible emergency, we're about thirty north of Topeka, 6000 coming down. We've got a pro-peller running wild here . . . looking for a place to land."

Kansas City Center is the FAA controlling agency for this part of the Midwest. As I spoke to a controller in a darkened room looking at a radar screen, the normal procedure would have been to follow the plane's identifier number with my location, altitude, and request. As the gravity of the situation had now set in, concern for proper radio etiquette was more or less lost.

The fact that I reported a possible emergency versus conveying the common protocol of "We have an emergency" or "Mayday, Mayday, Mayday," would help me understand after the accident that my mind was struggling to accept the reality of what we were most likely facing. Being normally very calm in almost any situation, I never realized it at the time, but I was no doubt dealing with mild shock that I had to overcome if we were going to live through the night.

It was obvious to everyone that we had a real emergency. Like many things in life we face, no matter how hard I wanted the situation to change, there was nothing I could do to make that happen. Thankfully, the excellent controller and supervisor at Kansas City Center realized this and treated it like the real emergency it was.

All pilots train for emergency situations and landings, and the dedicated men and women who work for the FAA and NTSB have helped produce one of the best and safest airway systems in the world. Every emergency is always a little different, and the ability to stay calm and make rational decisions is what will often keep you alive.

The first thing every pilot is told to do in an "emergency engine out" is to "just fly the plane." What this means is that you trim the plane up to make a stabilized descent with an airspeed best suited for your particular aircraft. In our aircraft, the Comanche PA-24, about 90 MPH would keep you in the air the longest, and about 105 MPH would get you the greatest distance.

Above the racket, I again heard the FAA controller in Kansas City Center: "November-eight-five-four-six-papa, roger. What is your altitude right now?"

"What's that? We are 5,100, coming down. Losing altitude," I replied.

The prop was still running at a furious speed from my steeper-than-normal descent, and the engine began to run even rougher. At that moment, I made one of several critical decisions. Coming to the realization we were not going to make it to an airport that night, I made the painful decision to let the plane continue at a steep rate of descent.

With the darkness of the night and little-to-no horizon to focus on, we were legally still operating under VFR (visual flight rules), but, in practicality, the night could have probably passed for what is called IFR (instrument flight rules). Instrument flight rules go into effect when one has little-to-no visual reference and must rely on the instruments for navigation and airplane altitude control. In the darkness or when clouds move in like they did that night, your natural, kinetic senses can easily trick you. With no horizon to focus on and no definite ground references other than Holton, Kansas, to the east, this intensified the workload and increased the danger of rolling over or crashing into a ground obstacle at high speed.

After a few short minutes, the air stabilized and we could breathe. Fortunately, the fuel lines never broke or caught on fire. However, we would be just short of landing before the smoke would significantly dissipate. By this time, any hope of a favorable outcome to this flight had quickly and cruelly ended. Like a petulant child, the plane was no longer responding as we continued our descent.

CHAPTER 13:

THE IMPENDING FACE
OF ETERNITY

My four oldest boys: Daniel, Matthew, Stephen, & Jonathan

SOON A NEW FEAR CAME to mind as the shaking intensified. I was afraid one of the blades might come off of the props spinner housing. If that happened and it did not go through the cockpit or further damage other critical parts of the aircraft, which was a high possibility, the concentric load of the remaining two blades would shake the engine off the motor mounts and out of the engine compartment housing. If that happened, it would cause the plane to become totally unstable and un-flyable. At that point, we would be little more than a piece of free-falling aircraft wreckage.

KCC flight control asked for an update on my altitude. By this time, the instrument panel was shaking so violently that the only instrument I remember being able to read was the blurred altimeter. I could hardly believe we were at 3,700 feet! We had been descending at over 700 feet per minute, and far more quickly than I would have wanted. Just over two minutes had now passed since my first call. Although things had seemed to go into slow motion, the hourglass of life seemed to be passing quickly.

I continued to peer into the darkness hoping to find a suitable spot to land, but there was only blackness and the random blur of a yard light through the haze and fog. I stumbled in my speech as I asked KCC to check for any nearby airports just in case there was one I had forgotten, but I knew there weren't any close. Nevertheless, he was trying to do everything he could to help, and he mentioned St. Mary's, about seventeen miles to the southwest.

"I don't think St. Mary's is lighted. I have smoke in the cockpit," I repeated. "I doubt I'll make it to Topeka," was my next transmission, holding on to only a specious hope of a landing strip nearby.

"Topeka is twelve o'clock and twenty-five miles," reported KCC.

"Well . . . there's no way," I replied back. Reality was becoming apparent. And then, a few seconds later, again pressing the microphone switch on the control yoke, I announced, "We're losing power quickly here." By this time, the engine had all but quit, struggling valiantly to hold onto its last waning surge of power.

After I began pulling back on the yoke a second time—somewhat in fear and somewhat to maintain altitude—I had to face the reality again. No matter what I did, we were not going to make it to an airport that night.

One of my hobbies is WWII history. General Patton is known to have said, "You make and process decisions to the best of your ability on what you know at the time." During those minutes of sudden disaster, that was exactly the position I was in.

I eased off the yoke, allowing the plane to pitch steeper and increasing the airspeed as the wind whistled by. If there was a fire, this would hopefully put it out or keep it from spreading.

"Are you still on rapid descent?" asked KCC.

I don't think I ever answered him but just contemplated his question and what seemed like dozens of other decisions that were flooding my mind.

"There's a town off to my left here. I'm not sure which one that is. I'm going to head over in that direction," I reported.

The town was Holton, Kansas. Although I had flown by this town many times, the stress of the situation didn't allow it to register in my mind exactly where I was. I was still hoping to find a more illuminated space to land or to possibly use the wide lanes of Highway 75 that runs north and south through Holton. That, too, was a destination we fell short of; and as it turned out, it was probably fortunate. Had I been able to control my descent better and begin that turn sooner to the east, we might have made it to the well-illuminated Highway 75. However, it's also heavily traveled, and I would have been quite slow and low in altitude by that point. If I didn't like what was in front of us at that point, we wouldn't have had much chance to deviate to an alternate landing spot. Driving on that road sometime later, I noticed that there is scarcely a quarter of a mile of that road that is not crossed with wires. At night, they would have been all but impossible to see.

The gravity of the moment was on my mind. In the brief minute preceding, I pretty much reconciled myself to the idea that we would not live through this event. I had made a decision to follow Christ's leading at an early point in my life. Although I was not eager to die, from the initial first shock and realization of what we were about to face, there was an unexplainable peace that came over me. If you have never experienced it, it is hard to explain. At the same time, I was grieved that I wouldn't be there for my kids or grandchildren. There was no time to say good-bye to my wife. I had been successful in business, but what value was that to me now?

Thoughts of my passengers flashed in my mind. Although I felt secure and at peace about where I would be in a few moments, I wondered where they were headed in eternity. I knew Steve well and knew where he stood with his faith; but I had only been with Paul for the past two days, and I never took the time to share the hope I had. It was too late now, and there was nothing I could do to change that. As my mind raced, there was a burdening sadness for those that I had met in life who might not share the peace I had. I was not only responsible for my life, but also for the lives of those in the plane, their families, loved ones, and those they had influenced.

You never want to be faced with that type of crisis; but when you have a relationship with God, it can be all we need and all we should want. Proverbs 16:9 reads, "The heart of man plans his way, but the Lord establishes his steps." When all of our plans fail and we have nowhere to go, God's guidance is all we have. That was the case that dark and lonely night in August when we all stared into the face of eternity.

CHAPTER 14:

DIM LIGHTS OF HOPE IN THE DARKNESS

Dim lights of guidance

AFTER I REALIZED WE WERE around 3,700 MSL—a measurement based on sea level—I never really focused on the instruments again. It was a strange thing for an instrument pilot in an emergency to do, but none of them were very useful to me from that point on.

As I strained to see out my side window into the darkness, there was nothing but the occasional dim yard lights. There was an exceptionally large unlit area below us, and as I peered into the space I caught a slight glimmer of light reflecting off the surface—a lake?

For a brief moment, I considered the thought of a water landing, but most Kansas lakes are isolated and sparsely populated, so there would be no one nearby if we needed assistance. Furthermore, the lakes are usually small, often filled with dams and dead trees. I judged that the odds of pulling off such a landing at night without flipping were not very promising. And were the emergency personnel prepared for a rapid water extraction? If we were still alive but seriously injured, we would surely drown.

Agonizingly, I ruled it out and continued into the dark, velvet blackness, unable to distinguish anything, but praying that I could find a spot to land. At night, you have no depth perception, and I could only sense we were getting close.

I had listened to the Topeka Billiard Airport AWOS (Automated Weather Observation System) prior to beginning my descent and knew Topeka was reporting "winds calm." Nevertheless, knowing that our right strut was low when we left Mitchell, South Dakota, I had been paying attention to the wind and felt we had a slight tailwind. My plan was to land with a slight crosswind from the left, so I could lift up the right wing with low air pressure in the strut. I started a turn to the north, hoping I could use whatever wind there was to slow down our ground speed.

Just then, to my left, I caught a glimpse of what appeared to be a dim set of lights. They appeared in my peripheral vision, and I continued to turn toward them. As quickly as they had come, they again disappeared, absorbed into the darkness of night. Later, neither passenger recalled seeing those headlights. A local farmer later told us that cars normally never go down that road at that time of night. Many have told stories of angels guiding us in the darkness, and we may never know exactly what I saw that night. There is a passage in Isaiah 45:7 that explains it the best: "I form light and create darkness, I make well-being and create calamity, I am the Lord, who does all these things."

The presence of those lights helped me make an instantaneous decision. It was now or never. I aimed the plane for the direction the light had just taken—all in good faith that an adequate road would soon appear. We continued deeper into the darkness. I knew I was getting close to the ground, and I began to pull back on the yoke to slow the plane in preparation for a crash landing. I still couldn't see the ground, but my best guess was that it would probably be between 950 and 1200 feet above sea level, corresponding to the settings on my altimeter. This put us within 500 feet or less of the ground, and, in less than a minute, this would be the final flight of the Comanche. It would be over.

What seemed like dozens of decisions began to flood my thoughts. Things began to run in slow motion as my brain was flooded with every bit of adrenaline in my system. I didn't want to get too slow because when I did get close to the ground, I would have no airspeed left for last minute decisions if I tried to change my landing spot or landing configuration.

My last transmission to Kansas City Center was heard. "You might want to send emergency help. We're probably going to need it. We're 2,000, coming down."

The controllers later told me that they couldn't believe how calm I was. The reality was that I had help that night that no man could give. I don't think any of us were actually calm, but we kept our composure. In those moments, despite the chaos, I do remember feeling a clear sense of purpose. I didn't have the right to give up. I had to fly the plane to the best of my ability. That was all I could do. The rest was beyond my control.

As I slowed the airplane, my right hand was on the landing gear switch. Again, decisions flooded my mind. *Do I drop the gear and landing flaps to slow the plane or keep up my air speed? What if I see electrical wires?* The landing gear on a Piper Comanche is exceptionally strong. If we snagged any electrical wires, with the possible exception of a phone line, the gear might withstand the strain and could flip us over. I wanted nothing to do with a power line that would probably win that match.

With one hand still on the gear lever and the other on the yoke, we descended. It would all be over shortly. A million thoughts were speeding through my mind as I guided the plane, but, simultaneously, I was imagining the potential result. In a few moments, my existence would be radically different, whether I was uninjured, alive but injured, or dead. I was surely optimistic to even consider surviving. People don't survive this type of crash, and, selfishly, I wished for it to be quick and painless. Could I tolerate living as a quadriplegic or going through years of rehabilitation if I lived?

CHAPTER 15:

A CRASH IN THE DARKNESS

The tree line we went through

QUESTIONS CONTINUED TO BOMBARD MY mind. *What else should I do? Should I drop the landing gear and slow up more?* I decided if we were going to hit a plowed field, leaving the landing gear up might prevent us from flipping. Still contemplating, I made the agonizing decision to leave the landing gear up.

In addition to strong landing lights, the Comanche had bright taxi lights, strobe lights, and a beacon. That night, I had everything turned on for the final moments of the flight. I continued on where I felt I had last seen lights on the ground. An instant later, just as if someone had flipped a switch, a gravel road suddenly appeared off to my left. As fast as the glimmer of hope came, the shock of what I saw brought one final surge of adrenaline. To my left side, we were approaching the road at about a ten-degree angle from the right. We had come amazingly close to finding the road's center, but there were dangerous obstacles on each side. Rural telephone poles and electrical wires lined the road to my left, and trees along the fence line were overhanging the road on the right. I didn't have the time and distance to perfectly line up with the road, but the Comanche's almost 38-foot wingspan had little hope of fitting between the obstacles, regardless.

In the next instant, I processed every possible scenario. If I jumped the wires, I definitely didn't want the landing gear down, and there was no way of knowing what lay beyond in the darkness. Statistically, most people don't make it over the wire. If I sheared off a pole, I could cartwheel; and if there were sparks, it could ignite any fuel that might spill in the process. If I veered to the right, over the trees, I had no idea what was there either, but I knew the terrain in that area was rough and undulating. I decided it was better to try and deal with what we knew and let pass what we could only speculate about.

Sometime later, when the three of us discussed the situation, we guessed that we had had about three seconds from the moment we first saw the trees illuminated by the landing lights until our first impact. We will never know for sure, but we could all agree that there was precious little time. As the plane's bright landing and taxi lights illuminated the narrow country road, our only hope for surviving this night was with God's help.

In an instant, I put the plane in a gentle "slip" as we came down between the treetops and poles. This is essentially an awkward maneuver, where the plane is skidding sideways through the air at a slight angle. I depressed the right rudder and dropped the left wing. I thought that if I could skim along the edge of the trees, perhaps the upper limbs would slow us down enough. If there were a break in the tree line, I could drop the gear, level the plane, and force it to the ground, while laying hard on the brakes after a landing. I dropped the left wing close to the ground and tried to get as close as possible to the power poles without hitting them.

Perhaps we can have a controlled crash without flipping, cartwheeling, or exploding.

I skimmed along the tops of the trees, trying to slow our airspeed— already faster than our normal approach speed. The top branches of the Kansas elm trees proved to be more than small limbs with their size obscured by the darkness of night. Moments later, the right wing sheared off a gangly trunk of a Kansas elm tree cutting deep into the right wing. With the loss of airspeed only a few feet from the ground, the left wing dropped, separating the left tip tank from the rest of the wing and leaving only a depression in the gravel road—later to be a lonely reminder of our first impact with the ground.

As the plane pitched into an even steeper descent in the remaining few feet above the ground, there was no longer any way to control our final destiny, as I no longer had any control of the plane. An instant later, the right wing again broke off a second treetop and then a third in rapid succession as the right wing separated almost entirely from the fuselage. In a blink of time that later became a blur in the past, we were strictly involuntary passengers at the end of a horrific ride to the ground.

My best guess is that we first impacted the trees traveling between 90 and 100 MPH. Steve remembers limbs hitting him in the face, since the windshield had now left the plane. I can remember a close-up view of tree limbs and leaves illuminated by the plane's landing lights. Then there was darkness in the final moment of the flight as our electrical system shut down, and we crashed through the trees.

The last tree we sheared off is probably what pulled off the remaining portion of the right wing, dragging us back to the right as the wing was partially hung up in the trees. I always knew the Comanche have a sturdy frame, but I'm still amazed that it didn't completely come apart as we plowed through the trees. Numerous trees were broken apart, and I'm convinced that the series of impacts gradually slowed us enough that we could survive the crash.

The final impact was when the fuselage hit the ground. At that point, what was left of the engine broke loose from the cabin, firewall, and any remaining connection to the engine mounts. This twisted us to the right as the belly of the plane skidded across the gravel road. As we slid into the east ditch to my right, the plane scraped against the trees and stopped forever, facing north-north-east. The trees never fully went through the sturdy airframe of the Comanche, but regardless, it was forever, fatally damaged.

The last thing Kansas City Center heard from me was a transmission of static. A little over five minutes had passed from my first call. After that, the transcript of activity at KCC shows a completely one-sided conversation:

"What did you say?"

"Four-six-pop, are you still with me?"

"November eight-five-four-six-papa, are you still with me, Sir?"

"November eight-five-four-six-papa, Center. You hear me?"

"November eight-five-four-six-papa, Center."

That night was the final flight of the Comanche.

No doubt that controller, his supervisor, and others had no other conclusion to come to but that this had resulted in a fatality. They understood all too well the improbable chance of surviving a crash in the dark.

CHAPTER 16:

ALIVE

A wrecker illuminated the once proud plane after the fire department had cut the roof off.

FOR A MOMENT, WE SAT there in pain, stunned from the experience we had just survived. After all of the noise and adrenaline that had rushed through us during the previous five or six minutes settled down, there was silence. It was an eerie feeling of serenity. The terror of night had subsided.

Did this really just happen? Are we really alive?

Looking around me, I could see that the beautiful, glossy, red and white Comanche was an utter wreck. Along with my feelings of amazement and gratefulness that we had survived, I felt sick about the loss of the plane. Somewhere on the way down, the door had disappeared. It was completely gone. It had been designed with two steel rods, each about a half-inch thick and an inch long that slid into the jamb and held the door firm when it was closed and latched. This was to ensure that the door never came off during flight. If it ever did, it might hit the rear stabilizer in the process, damaging it or rendering it inoperative as well. Knowing this only added to my astonishment as to what had just happened.

The windshield was also nowhere to be found. Older planes eventually need a windshield replacement, and most convert to a one-piece lexan model. However, when we had our windshield replaced a few years earlier, my aircraft partner, Jay, did not approve of the conversion and wanted to keep the center steel strut that also held the iron compass. That was a sturdy piece of metal that apparently had functioned well for what it was designed for as it remained the only surviving piece of the windshield assembly. I don't know when it came off or what removed it, but I'm fairly certain that it kept a lot of tree limbs from destroying the cabin and the three of us inside.

My side window was broken out, and the entire firewall and instrument panel had separated from the rest of the plane. Headsets, papers, equipment parts, and debris littered the once-pristine cockpit. I would later find out that even our seats had broken off the rails that are bolted to the frame.

Looking outside the cabin, a lonely yard light pierced the darkness, allowing me a decent view of the wreckage. Still in a daze, I was dumbfounded by the sight of mangled wings and ruptured fuel tanks spread around us. As standard habit and normal practice, I shut off the fuel mixture, switched off the magneto switches, turned off the ignition switch, and turned the fuel selector switches to the off position.

It was quiet now. The evening air was still and heavy. The noise was gone, and there was an eerie silence. It took a moment for us to realize that we really were alive, but thoughts of what condition we were in quickly followed.

My passengers and I had not said a word to each other on the way down. I was pretty busy with communications, looking for a spot to land, and controlling the airplane. Mentally and physically, I was at my limit, and I am sure my passengers knew it. Additionally, I am sure there was some degree of shock going on with all of us. Now we began to assess the situation.

Paul, still sitting in the backseat, had sent a text to his wife during the few short moments in the air prior to the crash. His solemn, and only, message was, "Pray for us. I love you." Only time would tell if it would be his last. Sliding the phone back in his pocket, he had hoped it might survive should he be thrown out of the plane on impact.

His wife would not fully comprehend the gravity of what seemed as only a thoughtful note until moments later when the 10:00 p.m. news interrupted with a special report. Breaking coverage announced that a plane had crashed north of Topeka. She, no doubt, went through her own trauma as shock and disbelief gripped her, with the startling realization that this might be her husband, Paul. It was not until she received a call from Paul at 10:20 p.m. that she knew that he was all right.

Miraculously, we were not on fire. The fuel attendant that had refused to fuel us only two hours earlier played a significant role in our survival. Both outside fuel tip tanks were destroyed, along with the center fuel auxiliary tanks. Only the main fuel tanks with the little remaining fuel survived the crash with their flexible, heavy, rubber bladders visible but not ruptured. Some would call it coincidence or just luck, but God had His hand on us that night and had watched over our steps. His future plans for us were not to end that night.

Many have died in much less serious situations, but that night we had been given a gift. We had faced the certain reality of death and survived to tell about it. Psalm 115:3 says, "Our God is in the heavens; He does all that He pleases." Our lives were in His hands that night, and there they will stay until someday we finally do see Him face to face. But, for now, we were still alive.

Only moments before, we were all experiencing the shock of anticipated injury or death. Now there was a new feeling of unbelief and thankfulness as the reality of our survival began to register with us. For now, three souls would continue living.

CHAPTER 17:

HELP ON THE WAY

ON THE GROUND, WE WERE beginning to comprehend that we were alive. I wanted out of that airplane. My first instinct was to ignore the pain and get away from that machine that had not only almost killed us but had also saved us in the same night. I could tell Steve, in the right passenger seat, was in excruciating pain. He was conscious, but he seemed to be fading in and out, not fully aware of what was going on because of the pain he was experiencing.

As I gathered my thoughts, Steve tried to get a leg out of our only doorway onto the wing, but he struggled to accomplish even that and, then, couldn't move at all. Later, x-rays at the hospital revealed a shattered pelvis from his femur being shoved up through his hip socket. Undoubtedly, this occurred when the right wing finally collapsed from impacting trees and, eventually, the ground. Without question, Steve's injuries were the most serious and long-lasting.

Since we were not on fire, I decided not to try and crawl over him for fear of worsening his injuries. I contemplated trying to crawl out my shattered side window or the front, but I wasn't positive that I would fit through either of the openings. I resigned myself to sit and wait for emergency help. I could feel my body stiffening, and I hoped I would still be able to move once help arrived.

By then, Paul had the presence of mind to remove the phone from his back pocket and call 911 for help. He calmly, but very matter-of-factly and pointedly, explained to the 911 operator that he had been in a plane crash, and we needed some help. From his response, it sounded like she did not believe him. When she asked him where he was, he hastily replied, "I have no idea. We are in an airplane." I think she became a bit more indignant at this point, thinking this might be a prank call, and again asked for a location.

Frustration quickly overcame the calm as he replied, "I don't know where we are!" Had the situation been less serious, it could have been a somewhat humorous moment. Only a few weeks later, the decision would be made to add triangulation equipment that would have allowed 911 to pinpoint our location based on a phone call.

As it turned out, there was a homeowner just west of our final stopping point. We had slid just north of his driveway by about 100 feet. No doubt the sound of the plane crashing through his trees, along with the bending and ripping metal, must have given them a jolt. The sheer energy transfer, able to snap off the mature elm trees, had to be roaring. He later told us that it sounded like a semi going overhead with the back doors banging. People in neighboring towns later gave the same report. The plane obviously caused quite a commotion. With every landing light, taxi light, navigation light, strobe, and locator beacon turned on, we would have made quite a spectacle diving through the evening sky.

What seemed to take an eternity was really only about a minute as we sat still in the wreckage. By this time, the neighbor had made it out the door and realized there had been a crash. After going back inside briefly for shoes and a flashlight, a voice approaching from the distance called, "Are you all right?" The flicker of his small flashlight, searching the cockpit and frantically surveying the wreckage dimly illuminated the area. Again, the words came that only moments before I thought I would never hear again—"Are you okay?"

This man was a retired Army medic and EMT like one of my sons is now. He had probably seen his share of accidents and carnage through the years; however, I am sure the startling sight of an aircraft crashing in front of his home was daunting just the same. He later told us that he returned with a flashlight with the expectation of counting bodies.

Fortunately, he was able to remain calm for us. Overhearing Paul in the backseat trying to communicate with the 911 operator, the neighbor asked for the phone and gave directions to our location, assuring her that this was the real thing. His wife and granddaughter soon joined him to watch from their driveway. As I felt around, I knew I had some chest injuries, but I couldn't see any bleeding. I was incredibly thirsty and was afraid I might have internal bleeding or that there might be a bone protruding out my back where I couldn't reach. As it turned out, my thirst was most likely from mild shock.

Had we landed over the trees that night, we would have been in terrain with deep ravines and probably would have nosed into one, becoming a statistic. Had we continued gliding at an angle over the top of the trees like I had planned, looking for an open spot, the next area we would have landed was a steep hill. With a slower air speed, I would have bellied into that incline or nosed in, most likely flipping over and, again, meeting our demise either way.

After my last call in the air, the FAA had contacted the Jackson County Sheriff. The emergency services were ready and waiting, but after we dropped below radar, they didn't know exactly where we were until Paul called the 911 dispatcher, and the neighbor clarified our location. Later, we found out that we had landed on N road, a seldom-traveled country road just south of State Highway 16. This is about two-and-a-half miles west and about a mile south of Holton, Kansas, in an area with rugged terrain. Help was now on the way.

CHAPTER 18:

LEAVING THE COCKPIT
FOR THE LAST TIME

ABOUT SIX MINUTES HAD PASSED since we had crashed. The momentary solitude, illuminated by a lonely yard light in the distance, was surreal. As quickly as we had perceived it, it had come to an end. The faint sound of sirens in the distance split the silence of night with an ever-increasing shrillness. As the sound intensified, the reflection of red, blue, and white flashes of lights on the emergency vehicles could be seen in the distance, beginning to pierce the evening haze. As they crested the hill, the whole area instantly lit up. Still dazed by the events of the night still fresh in our minds, we were mesmerized by the sight of so many approaching vehicles.

My heart raced and a thought of fear again crossed my mind as we sat motionless in the road, trapped inside the cockpit. For a moment, time seemed to stop. *Are they going to see us, or did we survive a plane crash only to be run over by a fire truck six minutes later?* Apparently, the homeowner who had come to our rescue had the same thought. He ran up the road waving his flashlight and caught their attention. All was well, and we were safe again.

In seconds, the large floodlight towers of the fire engines illuminated the area. I never knew the exact count, but by the time it was all over, I believe there were two fire engines, four ambulances, three highway patrol cars, and numerous first responders. There were well over thirty rescue and emergency personnel at the crash site, plus the neighbors and ourselves.

The first voice I heard from the emergency personnel was that of a young fireman in yellow. Illuminated from the side by the massive lights of the engine, I could see he was completely dressed in all his fireproof emergency gear. He bent over, peering through the wreckage, and looking in from my left side where the pilot's window had been. "Are you all right?" he asked, now only inches from my face.

I found out later why he looked so surprised. Stephen, my third son, was a police officer in Lawrence, Kansas, at that time. It was a job to support his family while he finished his master's degree. That night, he was listening to the Highway Patrol scanner and later told me of a 10–40 x 4, Code Black (meaning deceased persons) that he remembered coming over the scanner. At the time, he had no idea it was for me.

In my short transmission with KCC before the crash, I had failed to mention how many individuals were on board the plane. The FAA at KCC had apparently relayed that we had a four-seat aircraft, and they were prepared for four possible fatalities.

Knowing Steve had been injured the worst, I told them to get him out of the plane first. However, there were many responders there, and they took care of all of us with amazing efficiency. There wasn't much left of the roof, but the Jaws of Life were used to cut off what remained, so they could fold it back.

The EMTs immediately tried to put a neck brace on me and were trying to figure out how to get me on a backboard; but the neck brace pushed on my chest, which had been damaged by the shoulder strap, so I took it off as quickly as they put it on, which I am sure frustrated them. I told them my chest was crushed, and it was putting pressure on it. So, after several attempts, they gave in. While they were working with me, other emergency personnel worked with Steve outside the plane.

I remember that they placed a heavy blanket over him to protect him during the cutting of the frame. He later told me that the weight of that blanket caused his already-excruciating pain to skyrocket. All I could think about, however, was how I wanted out of that wreckage. As soon as the roof was off and the coast was clear, I took a deep breath and simply stood up, surprising all of the workers and probably causing some of them anxiety. My vision narrowed from the pain. I felt a little flushed as the blood fell from my upper body. Another fireman peered into my face with a startled look and again asked, "Are you all right?" I am not sure who was more surprised, him or me, but I was vertical now, and I was alive.

Stepping cautiously out of the wreckage, they helped me walk on my own to the ambulance gurney. I knew that medical personnel would normally cut a person's clothes off in an emergency. Despite the exchange and pain, my stubbornness was still quite intact. After all, I was wearing my favorite shirt! Surprising everyone again, I pulled it off as soon as I could, regardless of how painful the motion was. Checking myself out, I couldn't see any bones or bleeding, but my ribs and sternum seemed to be somewhat rearranged from the impact of the shoulder strap. They asked me to lie flat on the gurney, but it was more than I could handle, and I adamantly refused. That position pulled on my chest and definitely let me know something was wrong. With me partially sitting up, they loaded me into the ambulance for a ride to the hospital. I had left the cockpit of the Comanche airplane (call sign: *November 8546 Papa*) for the last time.

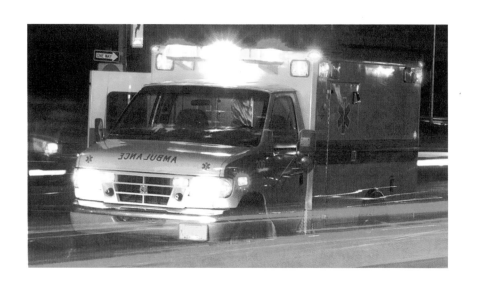

CHAPTER 19:

RIDING TO THE HOSPITAL

WE WERE NOW HEADED DOWN the gravel country road that, only fifteen minutes earlier, we had been trying to find from the sky above. Knowing the drowsy effects many painkillers can have, I didn't want the EMTs to give me any pain medication until I made some phone calls. I first called my wife, Suzanne, who was in Missouri, at the time checking my third daughter into college. The conversation was short. I told her I had been in a plane crash; I was beat up, but okay, and on the way to the hospital. I didn't want her to come home that night; there was nothing she could do.

The second call was to the FAA. I didn't have the time or patience for going through the answering menu to talk to the correct person and simply asked for a briefer. Typically, pilots call only for weather information, but after giving him my call sign, I quickly recounted what had happened and asked for a supervisor. A supervisor from another state came on the line and I repeated the story. Moment by moment, I was reliving the accident and the minutes that had preceded it, while still high from an adrenaline rush; and I am sure I was talking ninety miles an hour. I then asked him to contact the controller at Kansas City Center. "Tell him we are all alive and thanks for the help," I communicated in haste.

The last call was to Jay, who later remarked that it sounded like I was running on 150 percent adrenaline. Most likely, this was a true assessment. Jay was stunned by the news, although he was actually already headed to the airport. When a plane crashes, a piece of equipment called the ELT (Emergency Locator Transponder) automatically calls a preprogrammed number and emits a warning to other aircraft and the controlling FAA center for that area. Occasionally, if one has an extremely hard landing, the ELTs have been known to go off. Jay knew I had a low-landing strut and surmised that I had just had a hard landing, setting off the ELT without realizing it. When Jay couldn't reach me by phone, he assumed that is what happened, and he headed to the airport, thinking he would just turn it off.

Although I was trying to stay calm, the call to Jay was difficult. I had wrecked our baby, and, whether there was anything I could have done differently or not, I was still the PIC or "pilot in command," and I felt responsible. Pilots take pride in their flying skills and preparation, and I was no different. No pilot wants to be known for wrecking a plane, and I would have much rather been telling a story of how I had heroically saved the plane as well as everyone in it against impossible odds.

As I explained to Jay what had happened, the momentary silence said it all. He wasn't prepared or expecting this. He remained calm and was understanding but had genuine concern. This plane had been in his family since 1965, when his father had bought it new. His sons had all learned to fly in it, and a few years earlier, we had formed a partnered ownership to save it from sale with the rising costs of flying and maintaining it. This was its last flight.

Jay and I were already good friends, but this only brought us closer. Years earlier, Jay had experienced a similar circumstance with an engine failure in the same airplane from a crankshaft failure. To have an engine failure more than once in any aircraft is unusual at best. However, Jay's experience was in daylight, and he was able to get the plane down in one piece without any injury. The statistical chances of an engine failure are only about every 250,000 hours. To have two in the same plane, one by day, and one by night, is more than rare. Flying is still a safe mode of transportation, and I am thankful that this hasn't kept me on the ground.

I would have plenty of time to think about getting back to flying. For now, I was on the way to the hospital.

CHAPTER 20:

THE EMERGENCY ROOM

SHORTLY AFTER RECEIVING MY CALL, Suzanne called my third son, Stephen, a police officer on duty in Lawrence (about thirty minutes east of Topeka). Instantly, what he had heard earlier registered. It was for me and my passengers. He immediately told his supervisor he had to take emergency leave and sped to Stormont-Vail Regional Health Center in Topeka while still in uniform. He had no idea if I was alive or dead and, if I was alive, how long I would live. He almost beat me there and was joined by my son-in-law, Lance. They were the first familiar and welcome faces I saw. In the hospital, Stephen and Lance were huge helps in dealing with paperwork, greeting more friends and family members who showed up, and handling phone calls. When you come close to death's door, you gain a new appreciation for the importance of family and friends, and they are what really matters. Psalm 127:3 says that "children are a gift from the Lord," and that night, I whole-heartedly agreed.

Meanwhile, I was going through various tests and procedures. At one point, I overheard the nurses commenting that I had a fractured pelvis. *What? That's not me, is it?* It was actually Steve, who had been sitting next to me in the co-pilot seat. Steve had a fractured pelvis; they had momentarily mixed up the records, which was less than comforting at that moment. My son Stephen was there to correct the mix-up, and I was happy to not have an unnecessary operation. After the near mix-up about the fractured pelvis, I was even less interested in sedatives, thinking, *What else can go wrong in one night?* (I must admit, I, regretfully, was not the ideal, cooperative patient.) However, as the nurse and technician attempted to lay me back in preparation for the CT scan, I screamed as excruciating pain shot through my chest, and my vision again went black. I guess that is when I officially lost the battle with regard to pain medication. They didn't ask this time and only commented that I would feel something warm. As they were putting it in the IV shunt, my comment was, "Will that make me sick?"

"Maybe," came the ambivalent reply.

Great, I thought.

"Are you going to give me something that doesn't make me sick?" I repeated.

"Lay back please! You are going to feel something warm," they repeated.

We made it through the CT scan and x-rays, but by the time I was back in the ER, I had my answer. Hand me the trashcan. This was shortly after being greeted by Jay Hubbell, his wife Barbara, and his son Christopher. Jay and Chris are excellent aviators and good friends. It meant a lot to have them there, especially at that time of night. By now, it was shortly before midnight.

There were no major broken bones that they could definitely determine. However, there was a flight surgeon on duty that night that told me it is not uncommon to have fractured ribs and not have them clearly show up on x-rays at first. Consequently, I will probably never know the complete extent of the injury. Either way, all of my ribs were out of place, and it was hard to breathe. With my sternum indented on the right side, I could feel where the shoulder strap had been. Purple and red bruises appeared around my waist and diagonally across my chest where the strap had been. I don't remember releasing the belts after the crash, but I assume that they came off in the impact, which also caused our seats to break away from the rails that are attached to the frame. My spine had been lightly compacted, and that led to some later challenges. Follow-up visits to the doctor indicated that there might have been light bleeding in my knees that made it hard to walk.

Not long after the CT scan, a young highway patrol officer came to see me. He was very polite and, with a smile on his face, asked for my ID, pilot's license, and FAA medical certificate, which Stephen provided for him. I was cooperative with all of his requests until he asked if he could do a drug test. He made it clear that it was optional, but in that moment, the whole idea seemed impertinent. Not knowing this was standard procedure, I adamantly declared, "I have not been drinking, and I don't need a drug test!" I continued to declare that it was pointless until Stephen, my son of calmer mind, rolled his eyes, saying, "Dad, just let him take it. That way, there is no question."

Regretfully, I didn't realize it at the time, but I was still on quite a rampage, coming down from shock and my adrenaline high. I didn't like the idea or insinuation, and I didn't mind telling everyone. After being persuaded by clearer minds, I reluctantly agreed. Still complaining, they drew the blood before I realized it was over. As a CEO for many years, I suppose I was used to being in charge and getting things done my way. I was out of my comfort zone.

I never saw that highway patrolman again, nor did I see any of the medical personnel at the site, any of the EMTs, or any of the hospital staff again. I came in contact with over fifty people that were involved in taking care of us and making sure we stayed alive that night. They all worked the crash site with flawless precision and speed. Well-trained and dedicated, they all knew their jobs and did them well. I thoroughly appreciated all of their professionalism and efforts. Only a situation like this will make you fully appreciate what they do. It was an impressive sight and process.

Over three hours had passed since the crash, but what was ahead? Questions filled my mind as I waited in the emergency room. Was Steve still alive? How serious were his injuries? I had heard that he had been sent to Kansas City to a Level 1 Trauma Center by ambulance. Normally, this type of injury would have warranted a medevac flight to the Kansas City hospital. Fearing his reaction to another flight after our crash, hospital personnel made the decision to send him by ambulance. Only later did I learn of his disappointment when he was on the road. Finally realizing what was happening, he commented, "Why don't I get a helicopter ride?"

CHAPTER 21:

A NIGHT IN THE HOSPITAL

ONCE I WAS SETTLED IN a hospital room, the nurse wanted to give me morphine, and I kept arguing about how much he could give me. We settled on a small amount, although I really didn't know what that meant. As long as I was part of the decision, I felt better about it. I assumed that amount wasn't going to affect me, but before the night was over, I am sure more was given to help keep me more comfortable. I clearly wasn't used to morphine, and I had some quite interesting side effects—or so I'm told. Stephen's version is much more entertaining, explaining that I enjoyed directing the choir, raising my arms, and generally having a good time for the rest of the night.

I ended up spending one night in the hospital for observation. I was grateful to have my son Stephen stay all night with me and for most of the morning. The hospital staff finally agreed to let me go home before noon the next day, due in part, I am sure, to my boisterous, impatient behavior. I am sorry to say that my brain was running in overdrive, and I probably wasn't very rational or reasonable to those around me. It would take some time before I would fully understand all of the implications related to what we had been through.

I grew so tired of them asking what my pain level was that I just said one out of ten, hoping they would quit asking. What does one to ten mean, anyway? I was ready to go. By 10:00 a.m., the doctor on call came by. He never asked how I was doing or even really looked at me. Doctors are supposed to poke around and tickle you and generally be a nuisance. He didn't have a lot to say, but he just asked, "Do you want to go home?"

"Yes, I am ready to go!" I exclaimed.

I really wasn't, but I had determined that I would hurt no more or less at home than in the hospital, so it made sense to leave. Stephen rolled his eyes again, but the doctor never said much of anything else except, "Okay, we will see what we can do." After a long pause, he just shook his head and walked out.

By that time, I had had enough of the IV business and told the nurse to take it out. "Oh no," she replied, "I can't do that."

"Ok, I will take it out!" I said.

That got her attention, and, almost in a panic, she cried out, "Don't do that! You can't do that!"

Sure, I can, I thought.

I waited until she left and began unplugging things. Stephen just shook his head saying, "Dad, stop that!"

A few minutes later, the nurse came in wanting to know if I needed a chaplain. "Why, do you think I am dying?" I replied. She was momentarily silent and, with a "deer in the headlights stare," she shrugged her shoulders and left. It wasn't my intention to frustrate anyone, but, nevertheless, I most likely accomplished it. They were professional and trying to do their job, but God was still working out the kinks in my personality, and I still have a long way to go.

Many a close friend came to visit that morning before I left the hospital. I was overwhelmed by the number of individuals who reached out to me. Many in the world have no friends. Friends from church and business, as well as personal acquaintances showed up. Their care and compassion greatly affected me. They have been great examples of those who have figured out what is important in life. Before the morning was over, several dozen friends had shown up. Some even came the next day, surprised to find I had been released (or more accurately, had released myself). To those who came and those who continue to care, I will be forever grateful.

When the doctor and nurses still hadn't brought the discharge papers so that I could leave, I finally announced, "I'm leaving now." Barely able to stand, I had my hands on my hips, tubes still hanging all over me, and a dirty t-shirt and the dirty pants I had worn the day before back on. Stephen, half laughing and half worn out with me, said, "Sit down! You look ridiculous!" As the nurses ganged up on me, the conversation over the next few minutes went something like this:

Nurses: "You don't have discharge papers, Sir!"

My (seemingly obvious) response: "Well okay, then give them to me!"

Nurses: "We don't have them!"

My (authoritative) response: "Why not?"

Nurses: "We don't know where the discharge doctor is."

My (still-trying-to-be-in-charge) response: "Well, can't you find him?"

By then, they must have known I meant business and were probably ready to get rid of me anyway. I really can't say I blamed them. My intent wasn't to be obnoxious, but I just had not come down from the prior night's experience and hadn't figured that out yet. By this time, my pain level was increasing, but the papers soon came, and we headed out.

Steve, however, continued to spend the next six weeks in recovery. About two years later, he had to have a hip replaced.

Less than twenty-four hours had passed, and the reality that I was still alive had not fully sunk in. It would take some time to totally overcome the shock of this experience. I needed time to wind down.

The flight path through the tree tops and the remains of the aircraft

CHAPTER 22:

BACK HOME

THAT AFTERNOON, WHEN I ARRIVED home, I called Jay. He had already been to the crash site the night before. I couldn't relax as my mind continued to replay the events of that flight. *What else could I have done?* was the never-ending question flashing through my mind. I tortured myself for answers.

I needed to see the crash site, and Jay agreed to come by and take me. I hobbled to the car as my family members protested, and I, again, told them it would not be any more painful in the car than in my chair at home. I tried to hide how difficult it was to enter and exit the car. In reality, it became impossible to hide as I involuntarily gasped from pain with any extensive movement.

Once at the site, I was stunned. The road was even narrower than I had remembered, and there was a good-sized clump of trees that I had sheared off. Jay repeatedly commented, "I can't see how you survived what you went through." My mind began going into overdrive once again, reliving the event and asking myself, *What if this? What if that?* My brain agonized, grasping for answers. I am sure I replayed the flight a dozen times during that ride to and from the site. That was a pattern that would continue for some time.

Some of those answers came in the next few moments when the gentleman that had helped us the night before came down the drive from his house. After greeting us, his first words were, "It's a good thing you didn't try to land over there," pointing east of the tree line, where I had considered making a last-minute change. As I peered through the fence line and what remained of the broken trees, I saw the terrain was riddled with steep ravines and undulating ground. Even if the first contact had been on top of one of those ravines, the loss of airspeed would have dropped us head-on into the next embankment at probably no less than 80 MPH. We would have died on impact.

I studied the area up and down the road. To the south, there was a small country bridge in the bottom of the ravine. To the north, there were some openings in the tree line and, again, my mind raced, replaying the night before as if I could rewind history if I wanted to. It took only a moment to realize that the rapidly-rising terrain and the curve in the road would have caused a hard, belly landing. I would not have been able to fly up that steep of a slope and land.

I remember Jay telling me years ago of a Piper Cub airplane his friends had been flying. They were shooting coyotes and, after a hammer head stall at the top (an acrobatic maneuver similar to a 180-degree turn in the air from vertical to straight down), were unable to gain enough airspeed to recover. They pancaked into the ground and died five minutes later without a scratch. All of their internal organs had separated.

There were some other open spots, but all had random trees and obstacles. Had I hit a single tree, we most likely would have spun around or cartwheeled into a ball of flames. Had I controlled my airspeed better and conserved altitude, I would have overshot the road. N Road ended in a tee less than half a mile up the road.

After looking over the crash site, we went to the county storage yard, where a wrecker had moved the plane. As I looked at the plane wreckage, I was stunned that I could rattle the propeller blades back and forth. There are large races in the propellers' spinner hub that are around an inch or more in depth and width. The combination of the high speeds, non-aerodynamic alignment of the blades, and the lack of oil somehow completely reamed out the hub that held the large propeller blades.

On the drive home, tears welled up in my eyes as the gravity of the situation began pressing in on me. The adrenaline was beginning to wear off, and I was starting to calm down, processing things more clearly. In a few more hours, Suzanne would be home from Missouri, and I would see her again, my wife of forty years, mother of our nine children, and grandmother to our growing list of grandchildren. That chapter in our lives could have easily ended that dark night, but God had other plans.

When the freshness of this experience subsided in the days to come, I discussed with many people, including both Steve and Paul who survived with me, the amazing number of circumstances. If they had been only slightly different, they would have affected our survival. Some will always say that it was just coincidence and that we had had a lucky roll of the dice that night. For me, there were just too many things that occurred to accept that as my final conclusion.

There was little doubt in any of our minds that we all should have died that night. There was just too much going against us. Isaiah 41:10 says, "Fear not, for I am with you; be not dismayed, for I am your God; I will strengthen you, I will help you, I will uphold you with My righteous right hand." That was certainly the case that night.

When you survive something like this, the dust settles, and you look back, seeing the things that are important in life much clearer.

I will always remember my grandmother reading and making me memorize the 23rd Psalm as a young boy. Now, during times of stress or difficulty, it is the first thing that often comes to my mind. It says, "The Lord is my Shepherd; I shall not want" (v. 1). In other words, when there is nothing else we can turn to, He is all we want, and He is all we need. The writer goes on to say, "Even though I walk through the valley of the shadow of death, I will fear no evil, for You are with me . . . " (v. 4). When all else seems lost, most of the temporal things we esteem as important seem inconsequential.

Did I experience some fear during that dark night in August? I can't say there was no fear as we plummeted toward the ground. I don't think any of us would make that claim, but I can also say with certainty that I also felt the peace of God. We were in His hands, and I knew I could trust Him, whether we lived or died. That is a peace I have not always had.

The good neighbor that helped us that night later told us, "I think there were four people in there with you." As time passed, there was no doubt in any of our minds how true that statement was. God had saved our lives that lonely, dark, August night in Kansas. How that truth affected us was different for each of us. The future paths we would take were up to us, but we were all changed.

CHAPTER 23:

THE ROAD TO RECOVERY

I MADE IT THROUGH FRIDAY and Saturday night with the help of an ibuprofen and acetaminophen rotation with some hydrocodone added in. All of my ribs were still out of place, and it was difficult to breathe. My muscles had stiffened, and there was not a comfortable position to be in. For many nights to come, I tried to sleep in a chair sitting up.

On Saturday morning, I asked Suzanne to drive me to Philip Billard Airport, threatening to drive myself when she refused to take me. For many years, Saturday mornings have been spent at the airport working with young people, ages fourteen to eighteen along with many other dedicated friends and volunteers helping with Aviation Explorer Post 8. For a number of years, I have had the privilege of serving as an advisor, pilot, and President of the Board of Directors.

This program teaches teenage men and women about the wide range of aviation, gives experience in leadership, and for many, the opportunity to earn a pilot's license. More importantly, we try to pass on skills in leadership and commitment to community. This is a unique opportunity for young men and women to experience the broad field and opportunities of aviation. It would have killed me to miss Saturday's events, as this was

One of the yearly photos from the Air Explorers Squadron 8, BSA.

the 60th anniversary of the Post, and our hangar was filled with visitors and friends.

We are the oldest BSA (Boy Scout Association) Explorer Post in the world. It is one of only a few Aviation Explorer Posts and the only one owning two airplanes. This event was long-planned and the first of its kind: Alumni Weekend. It was great to see everyone, and I gave a brief run-down on what had happened. Almost everyone seemed concerned, but whether real or imagined, some were a little reserved that day, waiting for the FAA findings. I guess that is normal as most accidents are a result of pilot error.

After ground school the Explorers often wash airplanes to help raise money for the Post. This is the oldest post in the nation started in 1949 by Lt. Col. Charles Carpenter who wanted to do something to help youth.

Nevertheless, I enjoyed being there, and I had a long conversation with one of the fellow pilots who had a grandson in the Post. He had an interesting background. He retired flying 737s, but before that, he ferried small planes all over the world—talk about dangerous—back and forth across the ocean, when navigation and radio aids were not available. He is just one of the many pilots involved in this Post. Today, we have graduates that are all over the world. It has been a privilege and highlight of my life to be a part of this organization. I could easily write a book on the history and people involved in this organization, but that will have to be for another time.

On Sunday, against my wife's advice, I was determined to go to church. *I will just suck it up and go!* I propounded my new favorite line of, "I won't feel any worse there than staying here," and I hobbled to the car with the help of an old walking stick the kids found that had been my grandfather's. When we arrived, Suzanne said she would get someone to help me. "No. I can do it!" I said with self-reliant determination. I made it across the street without getting killed and headed down the walk to a class where we had made so many life friends. I could feel myself beginning to be a little lightheaded. I had to stop walking a few times, but I was almost there.

Backing out of the door was Jim Congdon, the Senior Pastor, who had just explained to the class what had happened and not to expect me. As he turned to leave, he stopped, amazed that I was there. After a few more hobbles, I made it to the door. Jim is a brilliant man and gifted pastor and teacher. I am proud to sit under his instruction on a weekly basis and to have him as a friend. When I walked in, the whole classroom stood up and clapped. I was totally taken off-guard and overcome with the love and concern they showed. (The adrenaline had long since dissipated, but it had burned a memory into my brain that would never be erased.) It was an emotional moment.

After the class was over, I got up to leave, and those around me said I screamed or shouted. It was the second, and only time in my life, I ever remember something like this occurring and reminded me of my hospital experience. It was hard to get up and down as it put pressure on my chest. My vision began to tunnel, and it took a minute for me to catch my breath. Suzanne was going to pick me up by the curb, but after a brief moment, waiting what seemed an inordinate amount of time (less than a minute in reality), I decided I didn't feel too bad, and I was going to go to the church service, which is located in a different building on campus. Across the long parking lot, I ventured, undaunted by pain or circumstance—I was on a mission! By the time I got to the lobby, I started feeling dizzy and lightheaded again.

Great, I thought. *I am going to pass out on the floor and get another ambulance ride to the hospital after I finish breaking what I missed the first time. Maybe I had better sit down.* Taking a big breath and gritting my teeth, I sat on a pew in the lobby. That is where Suzanne later found me. I had only temporarily escaped her oversight.

"Where have you been?" she asked with consternation in her voice.

"Just getting ready to go to church."

The service had already started by then, and that would be one Sunday I would miss. *Great! I have to get up again,* I thought. So, with one man on either side of me and with a big breath, they pulled me up and out of the chair. Limping off to the car, my demands to drive were met with little humor or sympathy.

"Get in!" my wife, Suzanne, asserted. Knowing I had met my Waterloo, I backed in, pulled up my bad leg and sulked all the way home. I was still running on an emotional high from the incident but unwilling to admit it, and I was physically running out of steam.

CHAPTER 24:

AFTERSHOCK

OVER THE NEXT FEW DAYS, much of my time was spent sleeping in the recliner or on the couch. I couldn't lie on my back, but I found a weird contortion, where I could put my arm behind my back and roll onto the couch for a little bit of horizontal R&R. Although I needed the rest, this was a low point in my mental and physical health. Formerly being always active, this was a new experience for me.

I was flooded with emails and cards from friends, as well as some acquaintances I hardly knew. It was overwhelming. Even on my kids' Facebook accounts, there were accolades of "Great job! Hero pilot! You saved everyone!" *What are they talking about? I wrecked the plane. We were almost killed.* I didn't want to hear it. It sounded strange and foreign. *Do they have me confused with someone else,* I thought. The heroism sentiments did not sit well with me, and it would take some time for that feeling to subside. I struggled with this for some months to come.

About midweek, my friend Dan Skoda came by to see me in the evening. Knowing he was an experienced private and military pilot, I immediately went into the technical specifics of the flight, rehearsing every detail. After he listened a while he said, "You know Dave, you might have some PTSD—Post Traumatic Stress Disorder." *What? Where did that come from?* That certainly wasn't in any of the John Wayne movies I had grown up with and had indoctrinated my kids with. I didn't have time for the luxury of (what I considered) feeling sorry for myself, so I passed it off.

Dan continued that he had a done a fair amount of reading on the subject and had been in required seminars related to his work. I remember hearing him say that with that much stress, it is almost like the adrenaline gland pops or bursts, branding our mind with the memory of the event. "Do you keep thinking about it and rehearsing it?" he asked. After a pause, I admitted that at least that part was somewhat true. Dan also encouraged me to write down everything that had happened that night, and I am glad he did. Much of what is written here is a result of that prompting.

I didn't think too much more about it, and I more or less dismissed it as something I would get over. Everybody has stress, and besides, I had been in business for years. I face difficult decisions, events, and changes every day.

The next evening, Dan's wife, Iana, called me on the phone, asking how I was, and I went into my speech about the technical details of the flight again. Both Dan and Iana are extremely experienced professional pilots, whom I highly respect, and I am privileged to have them as friends. When they were younger, they had their own FBO (Fixed Base Operator) at a local airport and had logged many hours of instruction. At the time of this writing, Dan is a Lt. Colonel with the United States Air Force's 190th Refueling Wing, flying KC-135 tankers. Iana is an airline pilot and mother of their lovely children. When Iana, with her kind and soft-spoken voice, suggested I might want to get some help, I thought, *Okay, they're ganging up on me now, but maybe I had better think about it. Only real friends tell you stuff like this.*

After months of resisting it, my attorney and insurance company insisted that I get some professional counseling. Although I only ended up with one (long) session, I finally realized that I couldn't let go of thinking that this was somehow my fault, that I was responsible for my passenger's injuries, and that, if I had somehow been a better pilot, this would not have happened. Our brains are complex organisms, and it is a strange thing, but it would take some time to get over feeling guilty about not being hurt worse than my passengers. In the months to follow, I found that this is not uncommon with many who have experienced similar situations.

After a less-than-ideal adolescence and being in business all my adult life, I was no stranger to difficulty. Therefore, I never had much patience for those who claimed to have PTSD or other similar ailments. To me, those who struggle with depression, or what is called PSTD in its many manifestations, just weren't willing to deal with the realities of life and rise above the situation. In reality, it was a naïve and uninformed assessment of what was going on.

With the help of patient friends and family, I realized that, at least to some degree, the crash had affected me. For almost nine months, I really didn't care if I went to work or not, until, finally, I was able to move on. Months passed, but, eventually, I was able to let go of rehearsing the accident in detail, contemplating endless scenarios and hypothetical endings if I had only done something differently. A strenuous exercise program, improved diet, getting back to work on a reasonable schedule, and the help of friends were key, but it would take more to help me move on.

A year later at our BSA Aviation Explorer Banquet, Capt. Al Haynes was our keynote speaker. When he was in Topeka, we had the privilege of having Al over to our home for dinner, and I was able to spend some time with him. Al was flying United Airlines Flight 232 in July of 1989 when he lost primary, secondary, and third tier redundant back-up hydraulic systems. With nothing but differential thrust, he was able to crash land at the Sioux City Airport. Miraculously, over half of the 296 passengers survived in an impossible situation. In multiple simulator attempts, they have never been able to successfully replicate that accident.

Al told us he had suffered from what is referred to as "survivor's guilt," often described as imagined guilt. Through professional help, he was able to move on, put the accident behind him, and eventually return to flying. Although the magnitude of having a commercial airliner full of people was completely different, many of our emotions were similar.

When you experience a traumatic situation, some people end up feeling guilty without being fully conscious of it. This was the case with me. Guilt is never something that God intended for us to live with, and it can immobilize us unless we learn to deal with it. It is an interesting fact of history, but a traumatic experience can often raise significant spiritual questions in a person's life. Most of us have known someone that has come close to death. Some of us, like myself, have stared it in the face, surviving to contemplate its implications.

All of us at some time have heard the words, "Why would God allow this to happen?" Many of us have asked that question ourselves. We may never fully be able to answer all of those questions because we aren't God, but I believe He allows certain extraordinary and distinctive circumstances in our lives from time to time to lead us to a greater purpose. Such was the case for me, as I considered more intentionally what the important issues of life were.

Without the help of my wife, close friends that stood by me, and a deep abiding relationship with a living Lord, I would never have been able to come out on top. Finally, I was able to close this chapter of life, accept the fact that there was nothing else I could have done, and put the aftershock of the accident behind me.

CHAPTER 25:

CONNECTING THE DOTS

Lycoming engine and the magnetos

EVERY RECIPROCATING PISTON ENGINE IN the class I normally fly is equipped with two magnetos, often abbreviated as "mag." If one fails, the other will take over. That is exactly what happened after our departure from Mitchell, South Dakota. Somewhere after takeoff (we assumed), the right magneto came off, and the left one took over. The problem was that there is no normal or standard procedure to check the magneto function once in the air, unless you suspect there is a problem or perceive a very slight drop in RPM. Since we didn't know until later that the right mag had come off, we eventually lost all of our engine oil through the small hole in the engine block.

An aircraft magneto is driven by the engine after the initial start by the battery. Along with a coil, it produces high voltage to fire the aircrafts spark plugs. They are common in piston aircraft because of their simplicity and reliability.

The initial investigation by the FAA shortly after the accident found the right magneto hanging in the bottom of the cowling by the engine plug wires. Again, during preflight checks, one can determine if a unit is malfunctioning, but in the air, the twin magneto takes over if there is a problem—as was the case the night of the crash. Unless you turned off the good magneto to find the engine faltering, you would never know in flight that you had an issue. Every revolution of the flywheel just threw out a little more oil.

For the months that followed the accident, the aircraft was stored inside of its own locked storage area at a secure hanger in an aircraft salvage yard. Numerous A&P mechanics, along with experts from Chicago and other areas, partially re-assembled the airplane's remains and removed critical parts for comprehensive and detailed inspection. Multiple attorneys stood guard, contemplating and discussing every detail of the investigation. To my knowledge, there was never a determination of product failure or defect.

I have been told that experts from the FAA and engineers at Lycoming (the engine manufacturer) estimated that it would have taken about one to one and a half hours before all of the engine oil was completely depleted through an open hole, where the magneto had been mounted. That was about the length of the flight from Mitchell, South Dakota, to our location, when the engine began to seize—and finally failed—north of Topeka, Kansas.

The nuts and washers holding the magneto were never found. Months passed before the initial findings were confirmed, and the FAA issued its final report. The report confirmed that the loss of the magneto from the engine block was the cause of the engine failure. Although the findings were inconclusive as to how this happened, there was strong sentiment that the magneto that had been recently replaced was tightened prior to adjusting the timing but never torqued down properly to prevent it from coming off. There is no doubt in my mind that this was an unfortunate oversight on the part of the mechanic, who could not recall actually completing this step when questioned by the FAA. Unfortunately, in life, unexpected things happen unintentionally. Nevertheless, this small deviation nearly proved fatal.

Why it took several hours to work itself loose is a question we will probably never answer. Various highly qualified A&P/A&I mechanics and experts in the field varied on the exact sequence of events that took place. Some felt the magneto came off shortly after or during our departure from Mitchell, which seems most likely. Some felt it may have been catastrophic, and, once loose, broke loose quickly, since there was little damage to the gears that engage the magneto. I agree with those that felt it probably came completely loose shortly after takeoff from Mitchell. No one can answer why it waited several hours to do so, but I am told that once precision nuts come loose from a bolt, they can roll off fairly quickly with the normal harmonic vibration of an engine.

Regardless of the sequence, all seemed to agree this was the cause of engine failure. In the providence of God, He had us where He wanted us. We could have just as easily been thirty miles further south and at the airport, or we could have died in a completely foreign area further north, but there was a different plan for our future that we didn't understand at the time. An Old Testament writer penned these words: "'For I know the plans I have for you,' declares the Lord, 'plans to prosper you and not to harm you, plans to give you a hope and a future'" (Jer. 29:11 NIV). At least for now, it was our time to go on living.

In spite of all those scenarios, this was another key in closing the emotional chapter on what had happened. There was nothing reasonable or in the realm of normal that I could have done to change things. It was good to have this resolution; we were finally able to connect the dots on what had happened to us.

The following is the final report from the NTSB (National Transportation Safety Board). This is what finally cleared me from any legal issues with the FAA and allowed me to move on.

NTSB Identification: CEN12LA551 14 CFR Part 91: General Aviation

Accident occurred Thursday, August 16, 2012 in Holton, KS Probable Cause Approval Date: 01/31/2013

Aircraft: PIPER PA-24–260, registration: N8546P Injuries: 2 Serious, I Minor.

NTSB investigators may not have traveled in support of this investigation and used data provided by various sources to prepare this aircraft accident report.

During a cross-country flight, the pilot and passengers smelled something burning; smoke began to fill the cockpit, and the oil pressure dropped. The propeller then over sped, and the engine seized. In the ensuing forced landing in the dark, the airplane struck trees and impacted a ditch. The engine was covered with oil, and the right magneto was found hanging by spark plug wires. The separation of the right magneto from the engine allowed the engine oil to escape, causing the engine to seize. The magneto had been installed in the airplane about 7 hours before the accident. The mechanic who had replaced the magneto could not recall if he had torqued the magneto attachment nuts. It is likely that the right magneto attachment nuts were not torqued properly and came loose.

The National Transportation Safety Board determines the probable cause(s) of this accident to be:

The mechanic's failure to adequately torque the right magneto attachment nuts, allowing the right magneto to come loose, which allowed engine oil to escape, causing the engine to seize.

Index for Aug 2012

Part II

FOR THOSE SEARCHING FOR ANSWERS TO THE DIFFICULT QUESTIONS OF LIFE AND CIRCUMSTANCE

CHAPTER 26:

DEPOSITS FOR ETERNITY

Flight 1549 "The Miracle on the Hudson"

IT IS HARD TO BELIEVE, but it has now been roughly forty-five years since I took my first real flight in a small plane. There was limited development around Johnson County Executive Airport (OJC) in Olathe, Kansas, in those days. The Gardner, Kansas Airport (K34) that we often visited nearby was a grass strip out in the middle of nowhere. Since that time, and to this day, I have never been able to get my fill of training or flying airplanes. There is always something to learn from others. There is always room to improve.

I find that learning keeps our minds young and active, as well as giving us the opportunity to help others. Our experiences are like a bucket; and when it is full, we have the propensity to let it out into the lives of others. That is when we can really start to make a difference.

Albert Einstein said, "Once you stop learning, you start dying." I would never want to take the credit for saving our lives the night of the crash. As I have said many times, there was never a doubt that Divine Providence led us through the darkness that night. Although far from perfect, I had developed enough skills through the years that God was able to use them to get us back to earth alive. Many successful people in life would share the same feeling regarding continuing a life of training.

Many great and far more experienced pilots than myself have spent their life training to be better pilots. Months after my accident, I visited my older son and his family in Charlotte, North Carolina. Airports and aviation museums have always been a magnet for my attention from the time I was a young boy to this day. When I heard there was a museum at the Charlotte Airport, I had to go. It was not until I arrived that I realized this was the Airbus A320–200, US Air Flight 1549, flown by Capt. Chesley "Sully" Sullenberger, that ended up making an emergency landing in the Hudson. Sully was one of those pilots with a broad background of experience and training that would one day pay off in ways he would never have expected.

This was a large commercial airliner with 155 occupants, so there was no comparison to the aircraft I was flying in relation to its size or passenger count. What was stunning to me, however, was how similar his thinking had been and how the FFA controllers handled that situation in the same professional manner. In his situation, familiarity with the area and experience allowed him to land the plane in the cold Hudson River, during January, without a single fatality. Consequently, it was nicknamed and became well-known as the "Miracle on the Hudson." By those that understand the obstacles he faced and the enormous unlikelihood of landing without loss of life, there could be no better title for this event in history.

When Captain Sullenberger was later asked how he was able to land this plane with only a few serious injuries, he responded with the following: "One way of looking at this might be that for forty-two years, I've been making small, regular deposits in this bank of experience, education, and training. And on January 15th, the balance was sufficient so that I could make a very large withdrawal."

We never know when it will be our time to withdraw from our experiences. Sullenberger went on to say: "I never knew that there would be 208 seconds on which my entire career would be judged." And so it is with us. We never know when our actions in this life will be judged. Most of us never take that challenge seriously as those seemingly urgent issues of life crowd out the important ones that we never seem to have time for.

Ironically, about a year later, I also heard Doreen Welsh, the head flight attendant, tell of her experience on this same flight, where she had served as the senior flight attendant. I again marveled at the calmness and fortitude that is often displayed under extreme challenges. This is another quality Sullenberger commented about, saying: "I practiced calmness so that when I needed it, I was able to force it into this extraordinary event."

Ms. Welsh sustained one of the more serious injuries, but she, too, was able to keep calm through years of training and experience. Losing a significant amount of blood, she continued to help others evacuate the sinking plane before being evacuated herself. Listening to her speak, she emphasized how important training had been for her. When there was a real life and death situation, that preparedness of training kicked in, allowing all the passengers and entire crew to live through the experience with minimal injury.

Even if we spend our entire life training in our field of expertise and interest, few of us ever spend time training for eternity to come. That night in August, I came about as close as you can get to death and still live to tell about it. All of us face varying crises here in this life. But after the accident, I had to ask myself, am I putting a regular deposit in the bank of eternity as I walk through the pilgrimage of life? Or do I live in denial, expecting that the present will never change and that I will live here forever?

All of us have known people that have died. Some die very young and some after lingering illnesses, and we wonder how they hang on. At other times, this life ends very unexpectedly. When the engine began to falter and then quit on me, I wanted to deny it, but the reality wouldn't be denied. After a minute or so, the reality of life's fragility flashed before me. No longer were there thoughts of tomorrow's work, relaxing at home, or projects needing to be done that seemed so important only moments before. I have come to the realization that whenever we reach that point in the journey of life, nothing will be more significant, important, or urgent than the decisions we have made that will affect eternity.

The days allotted to us do not respect time or status or accomplishment in life. We don't have to live in fear of the present or the future. That was never God's plan for our lives. There is something much better. Since that final flight of the Comanche, I often ask myself if I am making the right decisions and choices that will forever positively affect my future. Am I making a small deposit every day in planning for eternity?

CHAPTER 27:

EXPERIENCING PEACE

IF YOU ARE AT PEACE with your eternal destiny, then you have much to be thankful for. However, if some of this just doesn't make sense to you, and you can't seem to connect all the dots, this section will hopefully be for you. If you are not sure where you are, ask yourself this question: If I were to die in five minutes, what would happen to me? If you can't answer that truthfully or with conviction, hopefully the following will give you some answers you have been looking for, as it has for me.

If you remember, my grandparents raised me after my parents' divorce at age seven. It was a difficult time growing up, but they were a shelter and a refuge for me through the storms of family turmoil and the turbulent teen years. The week's schedule seldom changed, and Sunday was no exception. I always knew that Sunday morning's schedule was to get up and put on my best clothes for church, which usually included a tie and often a sport jacket or suit—not so uncommon in those days.

I attended a well-established mainline denomination, where the people were friendly, and church services and activities provided a good social time to meet others. I will never forget the huge pipe organ that bellowed out loud and complex music in varying scales and harmonies that would be followed by congregational singing and a message from the minister. I am sorry to say, I don't remember a single sermon that the minister ever gave.

Although there was no personal connection with God at the time, there was an awareness that Jesus had been a real person who came to earth for us. I can remember lying in bed at times wondering how Jesus could be a man but also God at the same time and how He could know all things. Often, I wondered, would I really go to heaven some day? My mind was filled with difficult questions of life. It was beyond my human ability to reason them all out. Is just trying to be a good person enough, or was there something else?

The following passage of Scripture has helped me answer some of those questions:

> Have this mind among yourselves, which is yours in Christ Jesus, who, though he was in the form of God, did not count equality with God a thing to be grasped, but emptied himself, by taking the form of a servant, being born in the likeness of men. And being found in human form, he humbled himself by becoming obedient to the point of death, even death on a cross. Therefore God has highly exalted him and bestowed on him the name that is above every name, so that at the name of Jesus every knee should bow, in heaven and on earth and under the earth, and every tongue confess that Jesus Christ is Lord, to the glory of God the Father (Phil. 2:5-11, RSV).

Jesus Christ was willing, for a time, to give up His throne in heaven over 2,000 years ago, so that we might know Him. But I had to come to the realization that it isn't enough just knowing about Him. He would never force Himself on me. That wouldn't be love. I had to make a choice—as we all do. When I chose to seek Him out and follow Him, I found the happiness and the meaning to life I had been looking for.

If we continue to choose only our own desires in life and ignore His presence, we will continue to struggle and wrestle with the difficult questions of life and eternity. Will we trust and believe in what He accomplished by dying on the cross as real; or will pride, procrastination, or the other pressures of life choke out a venerable experiential knowledge of all He has to offer?

When Christ suffered and died on the cross, He forever removed the guilt and sin of God's wrath. He defeated the power of darkness; no longer do we need to be alienated from Him. Matthew 11:28-30(RSV) reads, "Come to me, all you who labor and are heavy laden, and I will give you rest. Take my yoke upon you, and learn from me, for I am gentle and lowly in heart, and you will find rest for your souls. For My yoke is easy, and My burden is light."

He wants to give us rest from the pressures and uncertainties of this life, but it is up to us to ask Him. He will not force us to make a decision. He has promised that if we seek Him, we will find Him; and for those who seek Him, He has great plans. Jeremiah 29:11–13 says, "'For I know the plans I have for you,' declares the LORD, plans for welfare and not for evil, to give you a future and a hope. Then you will call upon Me and come and pray to Me, and I will hear you. You will seek Me and find Me, when you seek Me with all your heart."

If you have made a decision to follow Him and want to take the next step, then get involved in a church that uses the Bible as its main text. Find someone like-minded that has experienced this and talk to them. Don't focus on your failures and shortcomings, just keep moving forward, seeking who God is and what He has done. When you do, you will begin to experience the greatest adventures of life He has for you.

I am thankful for my friend George Granberry who, years ago, took me to hear about what having a relationship with a living God meant. It would have been easy for him to say nothing, but he cared enough to reach out. The day that happened, the reality of who this historic figure was that I had heard about in church for years became real to me for the first time, and I finally understood that He has far greater plans for our welfare than we have for ourselves. John 10:10–11 says, "The thief comes only to steal and kill and destroy. I came that they may have life and have it abundantly. I am the Good Shepherd. The good shepherd lays down his life for the sheep."

I am thankful that over 2,000 years have passed since that time He laid down His life in our place, and He still rules in the affairs of men today to accomplish His greater purpose. I am also thankful for those who took the time to share these truths with me. That is what brought me to a greater understanding of His presence, so that's why I didn't want to miss the opportunity to tell you. We all have a story to tell; thanks for listening to the one God gave me.

CHAPTER 28:

MOVING ON WITH LIFE

THE MOST COMMON QUESTION I receive after telling people of this accident and our miraculous survival is, "Are you still flying?" And, of course, the answer is "Yes." Through the years, it has become and will remain a significant part of my life until I am of the age that I can no longer obtain a medical certificate. The FAA never suspended my license during the investigation. After the conclusion of the formal investigation and report, the NTSB and FAA cleared me of any potential legal issues for any wrongdoing.

Due to my physical state and recovery after the accident, I first had a few rides as a passenger in the plane. Several months passed before I was healed enough from the misplaced ribs and bruises to fly on my own. After testing and letters from doctors, my medical certificate was reinstated, which allowed me to get back in the air a few months after the accident.

If I am flying for business or pleasure, I often fly the Aviation Explorer Post's Piper PA-28, also known as a Cherokee 180, a smaller version of my plane. I also have access to fly a Diamond DA-40, a Cirrus SR-22, and a PA-32 Twin Comanche on a regular basis. Because of the spare engine, both the Twin Comanche or the Cirrus with its ballistic parachute have some additional appeal—especially during night flights.

For the next two years, Steve still worked for the company but only for about thirty hours per week due to permanent injuries that he sustained in the accident. After a hip replacement, he decided to move on to start a new business. He now owns a successful leather goods store in Topeka, Kansas. Paul moved on to other employment shortly after the accident.

As for me, I am still active in the construction and development business, and I stay busy with many outside interests. I often joke that business is a distraction from my extracurricular activities as I am involved with several nonprofit, humanitarian, and ministry-related organizations. I am thankful for the dedicated staff and employees that stood by me through this difficult time and recovery. Their dedication and skill have allowed me time to share this story with you.

Recently, my third son, Stephen, who formerly worked in the real estate department, has rejoined the firm. Upon completion of his master's degree in business, he stepped into the retiring CFO's position. His increasing oversight of the family business will allow me to continue pursuing other interests that center around helping others. I have had the opportunity to speak to a number of groups and organizations about the accident and how it affected me. These include aviation groups, church gatherings, and civic groups. A common thread in these meetings is that it is a sobering fact when we all realize something similar can happen to any of us. I happened to walk away; however, many do not. At some point, honest people must ask themselves, "Am I ready?"

Generally, on Saturdays when I am in town, you will find me at Phillip Billard Airport's Hangar 15, working with young men and women to experience the joy, thrill, and opportunities afforded in aviation. Hangar 15 is the home of Aviation Explorers, Squadron 8. The Explorer Post has two aircraft fully dedicated to their use in giving youth an experience in aviation. So far three of my sons have received private pilot licenses there, and currently one more son is involved there as well. After the Explorer Scout meeting every Saturday morning, a number of advisors, including myself, take turns giving the high schoolers a ride in the PA-28 Piper Cherokee 180 or the Cessna 150 that is used as a primary trainer.

For whatever time I have left on this earth, I want to dedicate my time and efforts to helping others find peace and fulfillment in life and in their relationship with a living God that has sustained me and given me hope to go on.

I am also involved with The Navigators, an international Christian organization that played a pivotal role in my college years and through much of our married life. Suzanne and I desire to spend more time mentoring and encouraging others as they grow in their relationship with Jesus and also to develop workers for His kingdom.

Since the accident, I have also been able to come alongside organizations like TWR (Trans World Radio) as a consultant in Africa, leading a work project team in Bonaire. Only those who have come so close to death's door will completely understand, but I am thankful for whatever God may choose to do in and through my life in the days and years ahead.

I would also be remiss in explaining that keeping tabs on our children, their spouses, and our growing brood of grandchildren—that now outnumber our own large family of nine children—is no small task. We hope to be available for help and support as life brings its opportunities to them as well.

I have many hobbies that include skiing, boating, reading and continued study, woodworking, guitar-playing, and, of course, flying! In the years we have left, I also look forward to more writing, teaching, and involvement in the lives of others. Only time will tell what the next adventure will be, but I have learned that nothing is more fulfilling or satisfying than a life dedicated to understanding God's presence and purpose for our lives.

EPILOGUE

IF YOU HAVE MADE IT this far in the book, there must have been something that sparked your interest. Hopefully, it was more than an unusual story with a miraculous ending. Maybe you have stopped to think about how short life is and what is really important. For me, my accident brought me to a greater reality of how fragile a life can be and how quickly our plans for the future can change or come to a permanent end. Those of us who are older realize that few of us ever properly planned for the future when we were young, and we never carefully considered the fact that death might come when we didn't expect it or before we could live out our dreams and ambitions.

Isaiah 43:2 says, "When you pass through the waters, I will be with you; and through the rivers, they shall not overwhelm you; when you walk through fire you shall not be burned, and the flame shall not consume you." No matter how strong our faith in or our dependence on God is, He never promised we would not be subjected to difficulties or trials in life that come in many forms. Whether it is a harsh working environment, health issues, or an experience like we went through, others have gone through much worse. If we look to Him, He will see us through.

It is human nature to ask why these types of things happen. Later, in Isaiah 55:8-9, God says, "For my thoughts are not your thoughts, neither are your ways my ways . . . For as the heavens are higher than the earth, so are my ways higher than your ways and my thoughts than your thoughts." As a loving father regretfully disciplines a child, God, in His faithfulness to us, often allows difficulty, so we can come to grips with who He is. God didn't bring pain, suffering, and death into the world. That came from man's sin and rebellion and from Satan, the enemy of all mankind. God, in His love, sent Jesus to die in our place, on a cross of pain and humility, to take the guilt of our sin on His shoulders.

When we had our accident, we could have just as easily landed at Billard Airport or in a field without a scratch, or we could have made the extra few miles to the airport. But we would not have had the opportunity to reflect on the situation and the importance of our lives that God has given us. In the midst of life's greatest challenges and difficulties, seldom can we see any positives. My two friends and I were actually given a gift on that dark night in August. It was a time to refocus, reflect, and reevaluate what was important for the future. For many, coming to grips with mortality while facing eternity comes too late. The crash affected how we three men would face the rest of our future.

The end of life is often too unpleasant for us to seriously think about until we have to, and, oftentimes, we wait until it is too late. As life goes on, most of us have a growing awareness that one day our lives will end, but few of us live like we believe it. All of us know elderly or chronically ill people that we expect to die, but the reality is that all of us are terminal. The difference is that we may not yet know the method or the timing of our last days. The night of the crash, we all knew we were about to die, but as you know now, God had other plans.

We have had a chance to refocus our lives where we needed change. We have been able to consider how we spend our time and what would be important for the future. We have no delusion that we will live forever in this life, and some of us will carry physical and mental scars from that night for the rest of our lives; but for the time being, we have been given enough health and time to implement some changes in how we live.

On the night of the accident, I was as shocked as anyone else would be when facing the unexpected; but having accepted at an early age the reality of Jesus Christ and trying to develop that relationship for a number of years, I was able to be at peace. That doesn't mean that I wanted to die, that it had no effect on me, or that I wasn't scared. To the contrary, it was quite sobering; but if my life in this world had ended, I knew that I would go on living in God's presence for eternity. When Jesus raised

Lazarus from the grave in the Gospel of John, He said: "I am the resurrection and the life. Whoever believes in me, though he die, yet shall he live" (Jn. 11:25). This is the promise He gives to all who will accept it.

I also knew that if my life had ended, there would be no more relationships with those still living. I have determined that the things that last for eternity are few. Relationships are really all that matter in the light of eternity and where we will spend it. As the old adage goes, there are no U-Hauls to heaven.

If you have never really come to grips with what it means to have a personal relationship with Jesus, some of this may be more difficult for you to grasp. Many will tell you to "live for the moment," and some would agree to "live each day as if it were your last," but only for the temporary and fleeting pleasure of the moment. The temporal pursuits of money, sex, power, and all the pleasures this life has to offer will always come short of filling the void that exists in all of us. Our Creator, because of His love for us, has given us that void. Only at His feet, in the Word of God, will we find the answers to those difficult questions of life and a fulfilling peace. The famous King David once wrote in Psalm 16:11, "You make known to me the path of life; in your presence is fullness of joy; at your right hand are pleasures forevermore."

Let me encourage you to live your life so it will make a difference. Will you leave a legacy or an empty void when your life here is through? Don't worry about the past. As the saying goes, "There is no future in the past." Just determine to start anew on a worthwhile future path. Those who say, "Just one more day, and I will consider the claims of Christ or make changes in my life," may wait too long.

The answers to the questions that often plague us are worth searching for. When you find the answers, you will find fact, not fiction. It is like finding buried treasure. Matthew 13:44–46 says, "The kingdom of heaven is like treasure hidden in a field, which a man found and covered it up. Then in his joy he goes and sells all that he has and buys that field. Again, the kingdom of heaven is like a merchant in search of fine pearls, who, on finding one pearl of great value, went and sold all that he had and bought it."

If you are looking for that treasure, the following prayer of commitment is one that many have prayed along that journey.

Jesus, I thank You that You died on the cross for me. Forgive me for my sin. I ask You to come into my life, so that I can receive this free gift of God, which is eternal life. Amen

APPENDIX I

ASN Wikibase Occurrence # 147747

Last updated: 27 September 2013

This information is added by users of ASN. ASN nor the Flight Safety Foundation are responsible for the completeness or correctness of this information.

DATE:	16-AUG-2012
TIME:	9:50 PM
TYPE:	PIPER PA-24-260 COMANCHE
OWNER/OPERATOR:	N8546 PAPA LLC
REGISTRATION:	N8546P
C/N / MSN:	24-4003
FATALITIES:	FATALITIES: 0 / OCCUPANTS: 3
OTHER FATALITIES:	0
AIRPLANE DAMAGE:	WRITTEN OFF (DAMAGED BEYOND REPAIR)

LOCATION:	A ROAD 3 MILES WEST OF HOLTON, KS—UNITED STATES OF AMERICA
PHASE:	EN ROUTE
NATURE:	EXECUTIVE
DEPARTURE AIRPORT:	SOUTH DAKOTA
DESTINATION AIRPORT:	KTOP

Narrative:

Three Topeka men returning home from a business trip to North Dakota survived the crash of their small plane on a road about 3 miles west of Holton, Kansas, officials said late Thursday night 16 August 2012. The pilot and one passenger were seriously injured and the remaining passenger received minor injuries.

APPENDIX II

JUST FOR PILOTS SECTION:
Safety Recommendations I Learned from this
Experience that might SAVE YOUR LIFE

The following information will not be new or unfamiliar to either the experienced or the non-professional pilot like myself. It is also far from comprehensive. Nevertheless, these are a few bullet points that were reinforced in my mind as important. Proper preparedness and training at the right time might save a life, so I have included them for those that may have an interest.

My very first commercial flight was on a non-pressurized DC-3. As a youth, my father took me on a one and only business trip by air. He hated airplanes and later in life, he would never ride with me.

1. Situational Awareness
   - Always know where you are. What is the nearest airport?
   - What is the glide ratio of my aircraft? At my present altitude, how far can I glide under normal conditions?
2. Radio Communications
   - Keep ATCC, 121.5, or an appropriate frequency for ATC always dialed in case you need emergency help quickly.

- If you are a non-IFR rated pilot, learn how to use "Flight Following" and how to communicate with Center, so you are not intimidated if you have a need.

3. Cockpit Crew Management
   - If you have a pilot along, even a low time pilot, take a minute to discuss what you want him to do in case of an emergency and what his responsibilities are and are not.
   - Have him assist in navigation and keeping track of the next landing spot and that airport's frequency for an emergency situation.

4. Know Your Equipment
   - If you have a GPS or only an OBS, know how to determine your location quickly and how to find the nearest airport and get it into your flight plan.
   - Know how to find critical frequencies and keep them in your system.
   - Know how to use the radio control module and its features; many pilots do not.

5. Fly Within Your Ability
   - Don't fly in conditions that stretch the limits of your ability. When things don't go as planned, many have died when situations beyond their control caused them to lose control.

I have been an instrument rated pilot for a number of years and was capable of flying that night, but there was

Through the years I have had the privilege of logging time on dozens of aircraft. One of the most memorable flights I was ever able to take was in the WWII vintage B-17 Flying Fortress shown above.

a time I would not have been.

6. Manage Your Risk

- Our night landing had everything working against us—overcast, no moon or stars to give even partial illumination, haze in the air, ground fog, and a remote part of the state sparsely lit. I often tell the students in the Explorer Post that when there is a full moon, it is the best time to practice night flight.

- I try to avoid night flight in the conditions we were in, but if it happens due to delays, don't fly in these conditions in a single-engine plane. Staying at an alternate airport pilot lounge for the night may not be your idea of a good time, but remember all these add up to good stories for the future, and you can live to tell about it.

Top: My dad's brother, my Uncle Don Osborne, making his 1000th landing as a WWII Navy carrier pilot.

Bottom: Me in the cockpit of the same type of aircraft, a Grumman TBM Avenger, heavy torpedo bomber. Only a few of these aircraft remain.

- I don't fly IFR when it is down to minimum either, unless it happens beyond my control. Everyone has to set their standards on this based on their ability and equipment.

7. Never Stop Learning
   - Don't be too proud to keep learning or getting instruction. No pilot has learned everything there is to learn.
   - Every pilot has something he can teach. We continue to learn by helping others to learn. When we do, they will invariably ask us something we didn't know, and that's how we stay sharp.

Flying has been one of my life's greatest thrills and privileges, but it can be deadly to the one that takes it for granted. More than one pilot I have known pushed the limits when they knew better, and, sadly, they are no longer with us. Don't take chances with the precious gift of life. When life is gone, you can't get it back, so make the right choices, and you will continue to enjoy it for years to come.

HAPPY FLYING AND KEEP YOUR WINGS LEVEL!

Standing on the ramp outside of Air Explores Squadron 8's hanger with my youngest daughter Ruth. All of my children with the exception of my oldest son have been involved in this program and some have earned pilot's licenses through that involvement.

APPENDIX III

The following is a copy of the written transcript (transcribed by my son Stephen), documenting my conversation with Kansas City Center in those final minutes on the night of my accident. As a pilot, I have always prided myself on proper communication with the Air Traffic Control Centers around the country. One of my first instructors, years ago, always told me that if you don't want them to treat you as an amateur, then don't sound like one.

In reality, the FFA controllers have always been very helpful, professional, and courteous; and the night of our accident was no different. However, on the night of my crash, communication from my end, with mild shock, was hardly protocol, but the FAA controller was patient and as helpful as they could have been in that situation.

When a pilot declares an emergency, all other traffic is often diverted to a secondary frequency to keep the airwaves open, and full attention is given to the pilot in distress. I can remember that once all the other pilots on that same frequency heard the word *emergency*, the chatter became silent, and new planes joining in were redirected to a second controller. I can only imagine that this has to be a great stress on them as their workload increases with the full knowledge of knowing that there are people's lives hanging in the balance. A split-second decision or help from them on information needed may make the difference.

You can almost read the mind of the controller in the gaps of time wondering if there was something else he could do. At the end of the transmission, after impact, he called several times before concluding the inevitable. On the way to the hospital, I was glad that I could get a message back to them through the FAA system that we were all still alive.

A few months after the accident, some of the FAA employees that work at the Kansas City Flight Center volunteered their time to come in on a Saturday and give the Aviation Explorer Post youth I work with a tour. Kansas City Center is the controlling entity for all air traffic in the area of my crash, known as Prairie Sector, and covers a several state area. This gave the young men and women involved in the Explorer Post an opportunity to see the state of the art facility and be hands-on in real life situations.

Out of the hundreds of employees that work there, and not by any coincidence in my mind, I was assigned to the very sector that I had been flying on the night of my crash. Both the controller and his supervisor also happened to be on duty that day, and I was grateful to be able to tell them thank you for their help and to discuss briefly what happened that night. Here is a copy of our conversation during the final flight of the Comanche.

To the non-pilot, this transmission may be gripping, which it was. To the experienced pilot, the transmission back and forth and the accelerated descent were far from perfect. With the stress and shock of the unexpected and the many decisions that had to be made and considered, I am thankful to have walked away. Later calculations tell me that had I ignored the possibility of fire. If I had preserved the maximum amount of altitude, I still would have landed a few miles short of Billard Airport with no power and limited control.

Had we attempted to land at Mesa Verde, an unlighted airport with a grass runway, mentioned by the controller, it is very likely that we would not have found the airport and probably would have come short, crashing into a populated area. Several years ago, the commander of the 190th refueling wing had died at that airport by hitting the trees in a small plane. It would not be our landing spot. On that night, Divine Providence overshadowed our mistakes and inability.

The following is very close to a word-for-word translation with only minor grammatical edits for readability.

The following is a transcript of transmissions between Pilot David F. Osborne, Comanche N8546P, and FAA's Kansas City Flight Service Center (KCC) recorded on Thursday, August 16, 2012, at approximately 2138 hours Central Time.

The below timeline is noted as time marks on the audio recording only, not actual time.

Total time between beginning of first transmission and end of last transmission: 4min, 56sec.

Estimated time between prop running wild and impact: 5min, 38sec.

07:09—Osborne First Transmission: Kansas City Center, Comanche 8546P

07:22—KCC: Somebody else is checking on. Who's that?

07:44—KCC: Some Comanche was calling the Center. Who was it?

07:47—Osborne: Comanche eight-five-four-six-papa. We've got possible emergency here. Stand by please.

08:04—Osborne: Comanche eight-five-four-six-papa, Kansas City Center, we're about 50 north of Topeka. We've got a propeller running wild here. Gotta see if we can find an airstrip.

08:20—KCC: November-eight-five-four-six-papa, Roger. What is your altitude right now?

08:24—Osborne: What's that? We are 5100, coming down. Losing altitude.

08:30—KCC: November-eight-five-four-six-papa, Roger. Are you able to restate your transponder or you got too much going on there?

08:37—Osborne: No, give me a squawk.

08:38—KCC: November-eight-five-four-six-papa. Restate your transponder squawk two-one-five seven.

08:48—Osborne: Two-one-five-seven, four six pop (46P).

09:02—KCC: November-eight-five-four-six-papa. The . . . Topeka Billiard Airport is 12 o'clock and 30 miles, and I'm trying to pull up some other airports right now. Stand by.

09:13—Osborne: Ahh, we got smoke in the cockpit.

09:16—KCC: November-eight-five-four-six-papa, Roger. . . .

09:43—KCC: November-eight-five-four-six-papa, trying to find the nearest airport that's close to you there. Most of them are to the southeast by Topeka. To the southwest of you there's Saint Mary's airport, which is currently about 17 miles southwest of you.

10:07—Osborne: Is Saint Mary's a lighted airport?

10:10—KCC: November-eight-five-four-six-papa. Standby. I'm going to figure that out for you right now.

KCC—Unrelated radio traffic as the dispatcher transfers other aircraft to different frequencies to clear the airwaves for the emergency.

10:35—KCC: November-eight-five-four-six-papa. What is your current altitude now, Sir?

10:40—Well, we're 3,400.

10:44—KCC: November-four-six-papa, Roger. Are you going to be able to get it down to one of those airports or are you going to have to put it down where you're at?

10:51—Osborne: Well, I don't think Saint Mary's is lighted. I got smoke in the cockpit. I doubt I'll make Topeka.

10:56—KCC: And November four-six-papa, Roger. Topeka is 12 o'clock and 25 miles.

11:02—Osborne: Well . . . there's no way.

11:13—Osborne: Well, we're losing power quickly here. [*Engine slowing down in background is audible.*]

11:17—KCC: November four-six-papa, Roger. And are you still on a rapid descent?

11:40—KCC: Four-six-papa, Center.

11:49—Osborne: There's a town off to my left here. I'm not sure which one that is. I'm going to head over that direction.

11:59—Osborne: You might dispatch some emergency . . . vehicles. We're 2,000, coming down.

12:07—KCC: And four-six-papa, Roger. And . . . we'll . . . we're looking for that town right now. And we'll dispatch whatever we can . . . whatever we can find out, what is the closest town to you is there.

12:37—[*Radio keyed, audible static. Possible point of impact as the radio keys up.*]

12:50—KCC: [*Inaudible/broken*] What'd you say?

12:57—KCC: And our four-six-pop. Are you still with me?

13:11—KCC: November eight-five-four-six-papa. Are you still with me, Sir?

13:29—KCC: November eight-five-four-six-papa, Center. Ya hear me?

13:44—KCC: November eight-five-four-six-papa, Center.

15:16—KCC: [*Resumes normal radio traffic as other KCC workers contact the Jackson County Sheriff's Office Dispatch.*]

Minutes later, JCSO advises KCC the Sheriff's Deputies are on scene and the RP (Reporting Party) is the pilot (Osborne). JSCO confirms the crash with KCC and advises that the pilot and two passengers are injured. No fatalities.

APPENDIX IV

3 Topekans who survive plane crash ID'd
Engine trouble forced emergency landing west of Holton

Posted: August 16, 2012—10:15pm

ERIC SMITH/THE CAPITAL-JOURNAL

Three Topeka men survived the crash of this small plane Thursday night after the plane was forced to attempt an emergency landing west of Holton.

Related Stories

- Phil Anderson: Pilot recounts 'miracle' crash landing
- Topeka builder home again after crash landing

By *Eric Smith*

THE CAPITAL-JOURNAL

Three Topeka-area men who were returning home from a business trip to North Dakota survived the crash of their small plane on a road west of Holton, officials said late Thursday night.

The Kansas Highway Patrol identified the men as David F. Osborne, 58, of Berryton, who was piloting the plane; and passengers Steve L. Stutzman, 52, of Topeka, and Stephen M. Graff, 47, also of Topeka.

The patrol stated Osborne suffered disabling injuries and was taken to Stormont-Vail Regional Health Center in Topeka.

Stutzman also was taken to Stormont-Vail, the patrol said, and was to be life-flighted to The University of Kansas Hospital in Kansas City, Kan.

Graff suffered what the patrol said were minor injuries. He was treated at the scene.

TOPEKA BUILDER HOME AGAIN AFTER CRASH LANDING
Pilot talks of keeping his faith through long, dark descent

Posted: August 17, 2012—6:43am

THAD ALLTON/THE CAPITAL-JOURNAL

The wreckage of a plane that made a crash landing along a rural road west of Holton late Thursday night rested in a waste disposal site Friday morning. The plane was piloted by David F. Osborne, owner of DF Osborne Construction, whose skill in landing the disabled aircraft allowed him and two other passengers to survive the crash.

Related Stories

- 3 Topekans who survive plane crash ID'd
- Phil Anderson: Pilot recounts 'miracle' crash landing

By Phil Anderson and Eric Smith

THE CAPITAL-JOURNAL

David F. Osborne was back in his home near Berryton on Friday afternoon, less than a day after piloting a disabled small aircraft to a crash landing that he and two other men were able to survive.

Osborne, 58, owner of DF Osborne Construction, was piloting a small aircraft Thursday night, returning to Topeka with two passengers after a business trip in North Dakota.

Flying at an altitude of 9,500 feet, the plane was about 35 miles from its destination at Topeka's Philip Billard Municipal Airport.

Suddenly, around 9:50 p.m., the plane began experiencing engine trouble. The cabin began filling with smoke, and the small plane began a rapid descent.

Osborne immediately began planning for an emergency landing in the 1965 Piper Comanche single-engine airplane.

Jackson County Sheriff Tim Morse said Osborne thought he saw car lights on a rural road three miles west of Holton and planned his approach.

Witnesses said the plane sounded like a semi-truck with its tailgate flapping as it neared the ground.

Traveling at an estimated 90 mph, the plane struck several trees with its right wing before it landed on its bottom side in a ditch.

It came to an abrupt stop with its left wing extended over the roadway near 22625 N Road, about a half mile south of K-16 highway and three miles west of Holton.

Osborne and front-seat passenger Steven L. Stutzman, 52, suffered what the Kansas Highway Patrol called disabling injuries.

Osborne was taken by Jackson County Emergency Medical Services to Stormont-Vail Regional Health Center in Topeka. He remained overnight but was released Friday.

Stutzman also was taken to Stormont-Vail, then was airlifted to The University of Kansas Hospital in Kansas City, Kan., for treatment of what a friend said was a badly broken pelvis.

A third occupant of the plane, Stephen M. Graff, 47, of Topeka, suffered minor injuries. He was treated at the scene.

Osborne was in a great deal of pain Friday afternoon, but he said he felt much better than he did Thursday night immediately after the crash.

Seated in a leather chair in his home, where several family members were assisting him, Osborne said the plane began having trouble when it lost oil pressure. Within minutes, he said, the control panel "lit up like a Christmas tree."

He made a call to the Federal Aviation Administration in Kansas City to declare an emergency, then turned his attention to making a safe landing.

Osborne, who has been a pilot for about 30 years, said he stayed focused on flying the airplane and "making the best of a bad situation."

He searched for a place to land on the dark, overcast night, when not even the moonlight was available to help him see a safe place to land.

As the plane was coming in for a crash landing, Osborne brought the aircraft down on a narrow stretch of N Road, landing it between a tree line on the east side of the gravel road and power poles and lines on the west side.

"We're very thankful to the Lord for sparing our lives," he said. "We could very easily have been dead or paralyzed or injured a lot worse than we were."

On Friday morning, an owner of the plane, James Hubbell, 69, and his son, Christopher Hubbell, 43, both of Topeka, were standing on N Road, talking with Leon Conger, who lived in a house across the road from the crash site.

Conger earlier had told authorities the plane "sounded like a semi-truck with the tail gate banging" before it crashed.

After the crash, Conger ran outside with his flashlight and found the plane's wreckage. Amazingly, all three people were alert and talking. Conger then called for help.

Emergency responders were able to cut the roof off the plane and get the three men out.

The plane was owned by a limited liability company with three partners—the elder Hubbell, Osborne and Bill Leeds, a Topeka physician.

The elder Hubbell said he was notified of the plane's problem after its beacon signal was activated, indicating the aircraft was in distress.

"I thought maybe they'd had a hard landing over at Billard," Hubbell said. "As I was heading over there, I got a call. It was Dave, who was in the back seat of the ambulance, telling me the plane had crashed."

Christopher Hubbell said the plane's lights only illuminated a short distance in front of the aircraft, just enough to give about 1 or 2 seconds for Osborne to react before the plane hit the ground.

"He saw the power poles and swung a little to the right to avoid hitting the poles," Christopher Hubbell said. "That's all he had time to do."

Both Hubbells, who are pilots themselves, said they were amazed by Osborne's cool hand in what they described as "a pilot's worst nightmare"—making a landing at night with absolutely no light.

Because the plane was partially blocking N Road after it came to rest, it was moved early Friday to a lot on the east side of Holton, where the Federal Aviation Administration and National Safety Transportation Board were to inspect the aircraft.

Barry Feaker, executive director of the Topeka Rescue Mission, said Stutzman, who was the most seriously injured of the three occupants, was the former pastor of Open Way Church in North Topeka.

Stutzman also is a former employee at the mission, where he helped oversee construction of the Hope Center, a two-story facility for women and families, about 12 years ago.

Feaker said Stutzman, who also is a pilot, is now working with the DF Osborne Construction Co., which he said has projects in various parts of the nation.

The Rev. Mike Shinkle, current pastor of Open Way Church and a close friend of Stutzman's, said he visited Stutzman late Thursday in the trauma center at Stormont-Vail, before Stutzman was airlifted to the KU hospital.

Stutzman, he said, was in and out of consciousness because of pain medication for his injuries.

Shinkle noted there have been recent plane crashes in northeast Kansas in which no one walked away.

In Friday night's crash, he said, "there were 100 things that could have gone wrong and one thing that could have gone right, and that one thing went right."

When he was awake Thursday night, Stutzman praised Osborne for making a crash landing in extremely difficult circumstances, Shinkle said.

"Steve said Dave did an incredible job getting the plane down," Shinkle related. "The engine failed, and the cabin filled with smoke. It was nighttime, and they couldn't see where they were going."

Of the three crash survivors, Shinkle said, "They are under the hand of the Lord, to be here at this time."

TOPEKA MAN CONTINUES RECOVERY FROM PLANE CRASH
Stutzman was most seriously injured in crash west of Holton

Posted: August 23, 2012—1:00pm

FACEBOOK PHOTOGRAPH

Steve Stutzman continues to recover from a broken pelvis suffered in a plane crash Aug. 16 near Holton. The other two people on the plane also survived.

Related Stories

Phil Anderson: Pilot recounts 'miracle' crash landing

FIVE MINUTES TO IMPACT

By Phil Anderson

THE CAPITAL-JOURNAL

A Topeka man who suffered serious injuries in an airplane crash last week near Holton continues to recover at a Kansas City, Kan., hospital.

Steve Stutzman, 52, underwent a 5 1/2-hour surgery for a broken pelvis Tuesday afternoon and evening at The University of Kansas Hospital, said his pastor, the Rev. Mike Shinkle, of Open Way Church in North Topeka.

"He's doing well," Shinkle said. "The surgery went well. He's just dealing with pain issues now."

Despite the pain, Shinkle said, Stutzman was in "good spirits."

Stutzman was the front-seat passenger in a four-seat Piper Comanche airplane that was returning to Topeka from a business trip from New Town, N.D.

The plane was piloted by David F. Osborne, 58, of Berryton, owner of DF Osborne Construction.

Osborne was treated at Stormont-Vail Regional Health Center for injuries he sustained in the evening crash but was released from the hospital this past Friday.

Stephen M. Graff, 47, of Topeka, was the third passenger in the plane. He was seated in a back seat and didn't suffer serious injuries in the crash, which occurred about 9:50 p.m. Aug. 16 on a country road about 3 miles west of Holton.

PILOT'S SKILL CREDITED WITH SAVING PASSENGERS IN KANSAS PLANE CRASH

POSTED 7:17 PM, AUGUST 17, 2012, BY JASON M. VAUGHN AND TESS KOPPELMAN

HOLTON, Kan.—A plane crash north of Topeka late Thursday night still has everyone involved just shaking their heads in amazement after somehow everyone on board survived.

The crash happened last night just west of Holton, Kansas. The plane is badly damaged but all three men in the plane survived.

The front seat passenger was the most seriously injured—air ambulance took him to University of Kansas Hospital Thursday night with what appeared to be a broken pelvic bone. But the other two men literally walked away from the plane's wreckage.

"You look at that and can't believe they were able to live through that," says friend of the pilot and co-owner of the plane, Jay Hubbell. He had to see the wreckage for himself. He says his friend, pilot David Osborne did an amazing job piloting the plane to safety.

"I think a pilot's worst nightmare is an engine failure at night and off airport landing," Hubble says. "It's even worse with no moon and it's overcast so no starlight. So he faced the worst situation that he could."

Sheriff Tim Morse says the crash happened just before 10:00 p.m. Thursday, as the three men were returning to Topeka from a trip to North Dakota when the pilot reported that his cabin was filling with smoke.

"They lost their engine and they were trying to find a place to land but it was pitch dark outside," says Morse. "They saw some car lights on N Road so that's where they chose to land."

The plane clipped some trees on the way down and tore off the wing, but the sheriff's amazed that's all that went wrong.

"Narrowly missed a home, narrowly missed a power line," he says. "Things turned out pretty well."

The backseat passenger, Stephen Graff, had only minor bruises. Osborne was also banged up but walked away from the wreckage.

Front seat passenger Steven Stutzman was most critically injured, but friends are calling the whole thing nothing short of a miracle.

"Lot of help from the good Lord and a lot of skill as a pilot," says Hubbell. "He did well."

The only casualty is the plane itself, a 1964 Comanche that had been in Hubbell's family since his dad bought it in 1966.

"It's like losing a family member but when you get down to it as long as everybody is all right that's what counts," said Hubbell.

These photographs were taken of the aircraft remains in the county maintenance yard the following day where crews had moved it to in the early hours of the morning after the crash. This was the location that the NTSB investigated the wreckage and accident later that same day.

David and Suzanne Osborne with their nine children, spouses, and growing number of grandchildren at their home in 2016.

AUTHOR BIOGRAPHY

David F. Osborne grew up in Kansas City, the only son of Harold and Geraldine Osborne. Upon graduating from Shawnee Mission High School in Overland Park, he attended Kansas State University in Manhattan, Kansas, where he earned a Bachelor of Science degree in Construction Science from the College of Engineering and was awarded membership in Sigma Lambda Chi Honorary Fraternity.

After making a decision to seek out a relationship with Christ in his high school years, he became heavily involved with The Navigators, a Christian organization committed to helping others develop that same relationship. On August 1, 1976, David married his life partner, Suzanne. After finishing her master's degree in Speech Pathology, she became the mother of their nine children, which has been her full-time occupation since leaving her professional life.

Since his graduation from college, David has been in the construction and development business in the Midwest, as well as constructing and leasing back single-tenant properties. David remains active in the business world, but, in addition to family, much of his time is spent with an Aviation Explorer Post helping young men and women experience the excitement of flying.

David and his wife, Suzanne, are also involved in various nonprofit organizations, encompassing both local and international ministry opportunities. They remain active in their local church.